T0116924

The Seven Sorrows

Bible Study for Catholics
What We Can Learn from Our Mother of Sorrows

by

Beth Leonard

authorHOUSE®

AuthorHouse™
1663 Liberty Drive
Bloomington, IN 47403
www.authorhouse.com
Phone: 1 (800) 839-8640

Published by AuthorHouse   01/12/2017

ISBN: 978-1-4490-5137-2 (sc)
ISBN: 978-1-4490-5138-9 (e)

Library of Congress Control Number: 2009912597

Print information available on the last page.

Any people depicted in stock imagery provided by Thinkstock are models, and such images are being used for illustrative purposes only. Certain stock imagery © Thinkstock.

This book is printed on acid-free paper.

TABLE OF CONTENTS

ABOUT THIS BIBLE STUDY

Thank you for entering into this journey with me. Whether this is your first Bible Study or one of many, I hope that you learn something new about Our Blessed Mother, the Catholic faith, and the inseparable union between Holy Scripture and the timeless tradition of our beloved Mass. Mary teaches us the Seven Sorrows and asks us to meditate on them because their mysteries contain lessons of life, memories of Jesus' ultimate sacrifice, a better understanding of God's inexhaustible love for us, and humbling examples of Mary's perpetual faith.

For this study you will need a Catholic Bible. I used the New American Bible with Revised New Testament and Revised Psalms (NAB) which can be found in book stores or online at the United States Conference of Catholic Bishop's web site: http://www.usccb.org/bible/books-of-the-bible/index.cfm

Please note that even when using a Catholic Bible, there may be discrepancies in the translation and the verse numbering, especially with the book of Psalms. Look a verse ahead or behind if you do not find what you are looking for.

I hope that you are able to work through this study in your own quiet and prayerful time, but that you are able to come together as a group to share your thoughts and learn from each other's perspective. When a group of women volunteered to work through this study with me, we found that taking two chapters each week as our homework worked out very well. Those two chapters would then serve as our topic for group discussion on the day we gathered together. You can do less (one chapter per week) or more (the entire study during a retreat) if you choose. It is up to you or your Bible Study group to decide what best fits the schedule.

Author and Catholic Speaker information: Please contact the author, Beth Leonard through her website, BethLeonardbooks.com for Bible Study bulk book rates, to have Beth speak at your parish or for questions/comments about this book.

THE COVER STORY

The background story of the cover portrait of Mary

A true story of how God works in mysterious and heart-warming ways…

About two years before I wrote this book, and several months before I even heard of the Seven Sorrows of Mary devotion, I was given a great gift. It was one of those gifts that you don't realize right away. Although the planting of the seed was memorable enough, the flower it produced was far more incredible. I witnessed the artist at work as she painted this incredible picture of Our Blessed Mother… that was, to her, a huge disappointment!

Let me explain. Laura is an accomplished artist who decided to take a free-lance class to get a beautiful image of Mary out of her head and onto a canvas. She could have done the portrait on her own, as she owns her own fully-stocked art studio, but this was a serious endeavor for Laura and she wanted another set of artistically respected eyes watching over her.

What are the odds that she chose to attend the same class where I had enrolled! I was an amateur having fun molding a lump of clay when she entered our classroom to begin her new project. At this point, other than the instructor, the students had no idea why Laura had wanted to come to our class. She chose a seat in the back of the room where she quietly went to work.

One day, Laura was visually and audibly frustrated with her work. What was once a very serene and quiet workspace was now erupting with sighs and groans. We all raised our heads to see the teacher and Laura examining the portrait in front of her. Then the teacher asked Laura if she would allow her classmates to come over to see what she had been painting. Reluctant at first, then yielding to the teacher's request, Laura agreed.

I immediately rose from my table and headed toward Laura for I had been yearning for a glimpse of her work. The four of us in the room gathered around Laura and for the first time we saw her portrait and knew immediately who she had brushed into being. To us, Our Blessed Mother looked so beautiful, however, to Laura the painted image gave her great concern.

She was so frustrated with the paint. Nothing was going her way. In the upper left hand corner the paint was sticky and thick, like paste. The glob had no intention of spreading, as she would swirl her brush through the sticky mass. In stark contrast, however, under each eye, the paint kept running. We would watch Laura wipe the soft curve clean, only for the paint drips to slowly reappear. Laura was beside herself with disappointment and frustration. What was happening to her painting?

The optimist in the group finally spoke up. "Laura, leave it the way it is; maybe they are tears." But, clearly this was not the picture Laura had come to class to paint and it certainly was not the expression she had hoped to reveal. Laura disappointedly and rightfully replied, "Who wants to see Mary crying?"

She had a point. How many pictures do we see of a weeping Blessed Mother? Most art reveals her as a peaceful yet strong woman with a compassionate heart and a beautiful contemplative reverence. Mary is almost always portrayed with a welcoming and pleasant posture, willing to listen and to help us. When we see a person who is overcome with sorrow they seem less approachable and isolated from others around them. Sure, we have all experienced these moments, but our crying episodes are definitely not the moment-in-time picture we want captured and then hung on the walls of our homes.

We all went back to our places and I soon forgot about the painting.

Several months later, I found the prayer card that led me to a daily devotion of the Seven Sorrows of Mary and one year after, I decided to write a Bible Study for a small group of women to share. Funny thing, Laura was actually among the first group of women to participate in the reading of the manuscript that later became this book. The relevance of the portrait depicting the weeping Mary never entered our minds.

Flash-forward about two years from the classroom episode: The publisher's questionnaire asked if I would like to submit any artwork for consideration on the cover. Suddenly, prompted by the question, I thought of Laura. Still not remembering the exact picture, but hearing through friends that she had painted several very beautiful portraits of Mary since I last saw her, I thought I would give her a call. She met with me to discuss the options and had several pictures in tow—but not the one I saw her paint. We looked through the lovely portraits and then I asked her about "the painting in the classroom." She replied, "Oh, you do not want that one. Remember the fits it gave me. The paint was so sticky--- and then, do you remember what happened under the eyes?"

That was all that needed to be said. With vivid memory as if she had painted the picture that very day, we knew the blessing had come full circle. Of course! A book about sorrows needed a sorrowful portrait--- in fact, a portrait that would not have existed without divine intervention, or perhaps in this case, a bit of obstruction.

The painting was NOT what my friend had originally wanted to paint but it WAS the painting she was destined to paint. It was the painting that would draw us in and help us understand the sorrowful Mother who guides us through our own sorrows. It is the painting of a tearful Mother who just lost her Son, but gained for each of us a Savior!

The Artist of the Sorrowful Mother—Laura Liotti (see Acknowledgments page for more information)

DEDICATION

To Bill, Sarah and Moira.

Thank you for sharing your faith with me
and allowing me to see God's love through your love.

To my nana, mom and dad who passed on their love of our Blessed Mother to me.

For the Catholic Church, my moral compass and reservoir for faith.

ACKNOWLEDGMENTS

The Archdiosese of Indianapolis

Nihil Obstat: Rev. Daniel J. Mahan, STB, STL
     Censor Librorum
Imprimatur: Rev. Msgr. Joseph F. Schaedel
     Vicar General/Moderator of the Curia
The **Nihil Obstat** and **Imprimatur** and official declarations that a book or pamphlet is free of doctrinal or moral error. No implication is contained therein that those who have granted the **Nihil Obstat** and **Imprimatur** agree with the contents, opinions, or statements expressed.

New American Bible

Scripture texts in this work are taken from the *New American Bible with Revised New Testament and Revised Psalms* © 1991, 1986, 1970 Confraternity of Christian Doctrine, Washington, D.C. and are used by permission of the copyright owner. All Rights Reserved. No part of the *New American Bible* may be reproduced in any form without permission in writing from the copyright owner.

Catechism of the Catholic Church

English translation of the *Catechism of the Catholic Church* for the United States of America copyright © 1994, United States Catholic Conference, Inc.óLibreria Editrice Vaticana. English translation of the *Catechism of the Catholic Church: Modifications from the Editio Typica* copyright © 1997, United States Catholic Conference, Inc.óLibreria Editrice Vaticana.
Excerpts from the English translation of The Roman Missal © 1973, International Committee on English in the Liturgy, Inc. (ICEL). All rights reserved.

Merriam-Webster Dictionary

By permission. From Merriam-Webster's Collegiate® Dictionary, 11th Edition ©2008 by Merriam-Webster, Incorporated (www.Merriam-Webster.com).

Liturgy of the Word

Excerpts from the English translation of The Roman Missal © 1973,
International Committee on English in the Liturgy, Inc. (ICEL). All rights reserved.

Specialty Artwork

Artist, Laura Liotti, of Indianapolis, Indiana, has allowed her depiction of Our Blessed Mother to be used in this book. Her pictures include: Front Cover portrait of Sorrowful Mary and The Seventh Sorrow painting of Mary at the tomb of Jesus (page 65). Also, on page 57, is her personal photo of the Pieta by Michelangelo.

Introduction to the Sorrows

and what purpose they serve today

Sorrow 1: The prophecy of Simeon

Sorrow 2: The flight into Egypt

Sorrow 3: The loss of the Child Jesus in the temple

Sorrow 4: The meeting of Jesus and Mary on the Way of the Cross

Sorrow 5: The Crucifixion

Sorrow 6: The taking down of the Body of Jesus from the Cross

Sorrow 7: The burial of Jesus

THE SORROWS AND GOD

Mary, the mother of God, introduced us to the seven sorrows that pierced her heart and asked that we meditate upon their significance and importance. She taught these seven sorrows to St. Bridget who in turn shared them with us. We also meditate on sorrows found in the mysteries of the Rosary and, as we know, many holy people throughout time have used sorrowful elements of Christ's life to enrich and contemplate their own.

After studying her sorrows, mine seem small and insignificant. Not one of her sorrows is about herself. Not one has to do with a material thing. Not one relates to enduring gossip, a want not met, or hardship. It is not because she is poor or because she has been asked to do the unthinkable. She asks us to meditate because in doing so we will glorify God and will never forget the price that was paid for our salvation.

In meditation, Mary's sorrows deliver to us a more comprehensible view of God's own reactions. In other words, her sorrows are God's sorrows, but, because we know that God knows everything of the past and into the future, you might more precisely say that her sorrows were first God's sorrows. By meditating on these sorrows we first see Mary's heart, then Jesus' pain, and eventually the clear window into God.

Let's try looking at it from another angle. Have you ever felt that you could see God in someone's face or Jesus' pain or love in someone's eyes? If so, then maybe on a miniscule scale we can begin to understand what it must have been like to know Mary. Mary lived her entire life as the handmaid (or servant) of God, in perfect humility and devout selflessness. Because of these actions and the intimacy she shared with God, her being almost dissolves into a kind of transparency leaving her true love, God, illuminating through her.

Maybe this would be a good time to introduce you to the boxes that hold a "Catholic Link" to what we have been or will soon be studying. This link illustrates the connection between our Catholic faith and Scripture. We may find the link to join us to our beloved Liturgy of the Word (our Catholic Mass) or possibly to the pages in our book of Catholic doctrine, that is the *Catechism of the Catholic Church*. Whichever it may be, I hope you enjoy linking new lessons to ancient traditions and Holy Scripture.

Catholic Link

Catechism of the Catholic Church

4. Of all human persons, who most perfectly embodies the obedience of faith?

Para. 148: "The Virgin Mary most perfectly embodies the obedience of faith. By faith Mary welcomes the tidings and promise brought by the angel Gabriel, believing that 'with God nothing will be impossible' and so giving her assent: 'Behold I am the handmaid of the Lord; let it be [done] to me according to your word' (*Lk* 1:37-38; cf. *Gen* 18:14). Elizabeth greeted her: 'Blessed is she who believed that there would be a fulfillment of what was spoken to her from the Lord' (*Lk* 1:45). It is for this faith that all generations have called Mary blessed (Cf. *Lk* 1:48)."

Para. 2617: . . . She whom the Almighty made "full of grace" responds by offering her whole being: "Behold I am the handmaid of the Lord; let it be [done] to me according to your word." "Fiat": this is Christian prayer: to be wholly God's, because he is wholly ours.

God and Mary's union is unique. While she is daughter to the Father, mother to the Son and spouse to the Holy Spirit, you can imagine her bond. It doesn't get any closer than that my friends! Yet she continually reaches out to us in her obedient humility to reign us into God's fold. She is still working to please God and to save souls for the "A" team. I imagine that there are a host of things in Heaven that could occupy her time --- like having really fun parties with famous people and eating all you want --- but she seems to spend her time praying for you and me. She asks us to ask her to pray for us! Is she crazy, or is she simply crazy about God and what makes Him glow . . . a saved and flourishing soul?

Now that we understand that Mary illuminates these sorrows so that we may draw closer to God, let's look at the list of sorrows again and notice that the first sorrow began shortly after Christ's birth, happened again when he was still a toddler, and then at about the age of twelve. Different emotions are played out for us in these sorrows and we have much to learn from Mary's reaction. The first sorrow reveals hurtful news and anticipation while the second takes us through genuine fear and trepidation. The third teaches us faith beyond the emotions of anxiety and inquietude. The last four sorrows were compacted into one sorrowful and never-to-be-forgotten day. The day our Christ was crucified, died, and was buried. To gloss over this day would be missing God's most tender moments. To contemplate or meditate them is to know and understand, like never before, God's love for us.

WHY DO WE MEDITATE UPON THE SORROWS?

When we spend our time in meditation we are in essence filling ourselves up with God. We are taking the time to peel back the years of fogginess from the onion of time to clearly put ourselves back into the days of our Lord. The peeled back onion reveals to us what lies beneath the earth's dirt and the tough outer skin. The deeper we go, the better we can see all the way to the unblemished core. At the core of this meditation lies Mary's heart, pierced with the swords of sorrow, and the clearest window into God.

Meditating means to focus on something or to give great consideration to a particular subject of matter. It, therefore, allows us to refocus our day on someone or something greater than ourselves. Habitual meditation gives way to personal growth, fine-tuning, development, and mental refocus. Meditation is the stretching part of exercise. If we stretch before exercise we are less likely to injure ourselves. If we stretch after a long physical workout, it feels so good because the muscles are warmed up and primed. We can better isolate each muscle and give it the deserved attention. We tone and zero-in on each part as we stretch and likewise as we meditate. Our strength is increased through stretching as is our spirituality heightened through meditation. At the same time we are strengthening our soul, we are also bringing much happiness and celebration to all of heaven.

Think back to the last time you prayed for someone else and were consumed with his or her sorrow and pain. Our very nature tells us that when we move our thoughts to another we free up our own tensions and anxieties, allowing someone else's to temporarily take up residence. Without owning it, we invite it in to stay for a moment, an hour, or several hours and serve it, as if it were a guest in our own home. We so tenderly, delicately, and insightfully are able to understand their pain and our instincts beg us to console it...sometimes through prayer alone and sometimes calling for action. Nevertheless, we have put someone else ahead of ourselves and have benefited from the diversion of our troubles and the refreshed clarity at which we return to them.

For this reason, I believe Mary, through the grace of her Son, shared these times of tears with us so that we too might remember. Mary asks that we meditate on a sorrow and pray a Hail Mary. We repeat this until all seven sorrows are complete. Those who perform this devotion daily and spread it to others, will also receive specific graces from our Lady through her Son. There are no further instructions about the prayer, but I usually like to conclude the daily reflection with an Our Father and a Glory Be.

SEVEN GRACES FOR SEVEN SORROWS

a promise we can count on

Now this is the part that I had to read twice! I already loved praying to Mary so this devotion was easy for me, but the seven graces caught me off guard. Jesus and Mary ask us not only to meditate because it serves our mental being, but they honor us for this daily repetition with very specific promises of grace. To me, the next part merits a huge WOW! For not only do they offer this grace to us who recite and contemplate, but to our family! Call it what you like: "Icing on the cake," "Bonus #2," or perhaps the old, "...but wait, there is more!" Whatever comes to mind, know that Mary's graces are designed to protect, console, help, and even serve us along with our families. Can you think of a better offer? There is nothing to lose and so much to gain.

The graces are, as passed down to us from St. Bridget along with the Sorrows:

1. I will grant peace to their families.

2. They will be enlightened about the Divine mysteries.

3. I will console them in their pains and I will accompany them in their work.

4. I will give them as much as they ask for, as long as it does not oppose the Adorable Will of my Divine Son or the sanctification of their souls.

5. I will defend them in their spiritual battles with the infernal enemy and I will protect them at every instant of their lives.

6. I will visibly help them at the moment of their death; they will see the face of their mother.

7. I have obtained (this grace) from my Divine Son, that those who propagate this devotion to my tears and dolors, will be taken directly from this earthly life to eternal happiness, since all their sins will be forgiven and my Son and I will be their eternal consolation and joy.

Words cannot even describe the chill that I received as I first learned of these graces. I cannot describe what these possibilities meant to me. For spending a few minutes with Mary each day, I could receive such grace! Yes, grace not only for me, but also for the family that I love and would do anything to protect. It is the perfect gift! It is the gift that lasts long after we are gone from this earth and continues into heavenly eternity. It is truly wondrous what the power of these graces can do to those who place faith in them.

Which ones especially talk to you and why? _____

_____

_____

_____

_____

Underline one or two words in each that summarize the grace in your mind. Then try to memorize these graces by the words you chose. I chose peace, enlighten, console, give *for* asking, defend, visibly help, and forgive. Practice memorization of the words you chose by writing them here:

1_____ 2_____ 3_____

4_____ 5_____ 6_____

7_____

MEDITATION HELPS US PREPARE FOR BATTLE

We, who dwell on Earth, are expected to battle for our God so that we bring souls with us to heaven. Angels, although brilliant at fighting battles for us behind the scenes, must depend on us to win the earthly battles. As in chess, think of us as living pieces on the game board that must move strategically into position to overtake the opposition. Remember that God could, if He desired, take the guessing out of the game and move us rather than willing us to move, but that is not how God works.

Relinquishing total control to us for our own lives, he allows us to set our own pace and experience free mobility. If we, as a pawn, knight, or even queen, choose to move obliviously or deliberately to a threatening position, God will not intervene, and the game may take a sharp turn south. Other pieces may have to work even harder or possibly sacrifice their positions to keep our team strong. Because we work together for God, you can see how a few wrong moves can cause others jeopardy. You can also see that when we are moving thoughtfully and with God, we build up the power of our entire team. God counts on each of us to play our part and to strengthen His kingdom on Earth. When we are lost or misdirected, we can confuse the strategy and sometimes---even stand in the way of forward progress. God patiently watches our moves and awaits our "reply" for Him to be with us. It truly is a reply, not a request, because God never abandons us. He is always in the offering mode. It is we who must decide to answer yes. When we cry out, He picks us up and carries us back to safety. Then, after brushing us off, sets us back down on our own two feet to make our next move, hopefully with His guidance.

*Proverbs 16: 9 and 3 In his mind a man plans his course, but the Lord directs his steps.
Entrust your works to the Lord, and your plans will succeed.*

and

*Psalms 27:5 For God will hide me in his shelter in time of trouble,
Will conceal me in the cover of his tent; and set me high upon a rock.*

and

*Psalms 31: 9 You will not abandon me into enemy hands,
but will set my feet in a free and open space.*

and lastly

Job 5:11 He sets up on high the lowly, and those who mourn he exalts to safety.

If we listen to Him always, we will be more likely to make fewer mistakes. We must know that Our God is the mastermind behind the "Big Game" and He will win. He fights to keep even the lowliest or most insignificant piece from falling into the dreadful clutches of his opposition. As long as we let Him, we will see more victories than we thought were possible. Remember, too, that in chess, at times it may look like the game is over, when all at once the master's great strategy is revealed. We must always trust in God's plan and celebrate the victories. He not only wants to share the inevitable win with us, but He wishes to make us investors rather than simply inheritors of the win. Can you find the time to invest in His will and keep our enemy on the defensive? If so, can you hear a resounding "Checkmate" in our future?

Write below some ways that you intentionally invest your time in Him.

_____

_____

_____

GOD NEVER ABANDONS US

As often as we have heard it, "God never abandons us," and we want so desperately to believe it, we have also at times felt abandoned. Let's get some insight from the Bible so we can better understand this tug of war between feeling loved and feeling abandoned. Below are some Old Testament examples. Answer by circling if the author felt abandoned, loved, or both.

Job 7: 1-2	Abandoned	Loved	Both abandoned and loved
Job 10: 8-12	Abandoned	Loved	Both abandoned and loved
Job 30:20-21	Abandoned	Loved	Both abandoned and loved
Ps. 18:19-20	Abandoned	Loved	Both abandoned and loved
Isaiah 1: 15-18	Abandoned	Loved	Both abandoned and loved

Ps. 22: 2-3	Abandoned	Loved	Both abandoned and loved
Ps. 22:25	Abandoned	Loved	Both abandoned and loved
Ps. 23:4	Abandoned	Loved	Both abandoned and loved

Isn't it amazing? We are not alone in our pitiful pits and jubilant joys. Time has found no cure for the emotional polarization of life on earth. Jesus understood this emotional wrestling within man and spent his days on earth leading by example and teaching us about God's love for us. Then, before his resurrection, Jesus told us of God's promise fulfilled for us and promised us another layer of hope and security that will stay with us until we are called to heaven. Let us read Luke's account of how this gift comes upon us. Luke 24: 49.

Who is sending this gift? _____

_____

Who initially promised it? _____

_____

More like a security blanket of sorts, it is to be delivered _____ us, as opposed to within us.

This is important: Until they received this gift, what were they to do?

_____Try it on their own   _____Go into hiding   _____Stay in the city

How did Jesus describe this gift? *...until you are* _____

_____

Imagine that! We are walking around "*clothed with the power from on high.*" The power does not merely surround our church, community, or home. The power is not an invisible zone of protection that encircles us. This power is touching us as our shirt, pants, socks, and hats touch us and we should be able to feel the Almighty presence, not just have to trust that it is there. What an amazing gift from God. Our Catholic faith recognizes the significance of this gift and incorporates it into our very first sacrament. What is our gateway to life in the Spirit?

_____

Catholic Link

Catechism of the Catholic Church

1213

Holy Baptism is the basis of the whole Christian life, the gateway to life in the Spirit (vitae spiritualis ianua) and the door which gives access to the other sacraments.

REFLECT AND ABSORB

We meditate on these sorrows of Mary to understand and bring clarity to the Father, Son, and Holy Spirit. Mary, our advocate, has asked for and been given the graces that she extends to us, her prayerful warriors. Our Catholic faith is blessed by these great wonders and is filled with answers to some of life's toughest questions. The closer we look into the nooks and crannies of our faith, the more we are amazed at its beauty, reverence, and sophistication. We may struggle at times, and often we may feel unloved or abandoned by God. We may intentionally turn from God, but he will not leave us.

In the chess game of life, do any times come to mind where you were not moving in the right direction or failed to move at all out of fear or stubbornness? Perhaps we tend to move all over the place not always looking ahead or watching out for other pieces around us who might be in danger. Does misery love company or is happiness contagious? Think about ways we can and do prepare ourselves for battle and make note of them here before we move on.

_____

_____

_____

_____

_____

The Prophecy of Simeon

the first sorrow

Read Luke 2: 22-38 for context, and specifically look at 25-35 for the intention of this sorrow.

SIMEON MEETS MARY AND JOSEPH

Mary probably happily awakened on that morning knowing that this would be the day to rightfully present her son to the Lord. (The same Lord that had sent the Holy Spirit upon her so that she might conceive her precious son.) I am sure that she took great care of him as she prepared him for the journey.

Upon entering the temple, she is greeted by Simeon, a Godly and righteous man, who has much to say to the parents of Jesus.

Simeon divulged many highly confidential bits of information to this young couple, some of which they knew or suspected by the past greetings from heaven. Yet, we can conclude that most of Simeon's prophetic talk caught them by surprise. In verse 33, Luke states that *"the child's father and mother were _____ at what was said about him"*.

Amazed, yes! Jesus was to be the salvation for *"all peoples"* according to Simeon in Verse 31. And if there were any questions still left in their minds at that point, Simeon would continue and further clarify. Who was this baby boy to reveal light to? (See verse 32)_____ And who was he to bring glory to? (See verse 32)_____

This alone could have been somewhat puzzling to Mary and Joseph since the Messiah they awaited was supposedly for Israel, but this child would be for "all peoples," with the Gentiles specifically included. You have to remember that Gentiles meant any "non–Jew" and although Gentiles sought God in the Old Testament, they would be required to convert. Mary and Joseph's God was the God of David and Jacob. Their God, who allowed them great victories against the other kingdoms or "other peoples," was now to deliver a Savior to everyone! How would this be accomplished?

Mary and Joseph would not have had enough information to fully understand the breadth and depth of this Universal Savior and the New Covenant; however, they were beginning to understand that this was a much greater plan that was being brought forth from their Almighty God. This young couple may not have understood everything, but they had one thing for sure– FAITH, and that is what would help them through the sorrows that lay ahead. For these obedient children of God, these words must have set the stage for deeper thought and contemplation, (or possibly great conversation on the way home from the temple that very day!) What they had been taught to believe in Jewish custom, practice, and law was to be turned upside down. Some would rise and some would _____(verse 34).

The Gentiles were to specifically be a target of salvation as we see unfold in Acts 13: 44–49. Paul and Barnabas were addressing the crowds at Lystra when the Jews became jealous (verse 45). How did the apostles rebuke them? See Acts 13: 46 for the answer. _____

_____

_____

In verse 47, we are reminded of the prophesy of Simeon. The Lord commanded them; *"I have made you a _____ to the Gentiles, that you may be an instrument of salvation to the ends of the earth."* Indeed, Simeon's words about the baby Jesus' revelation upon the Gentiles had come to "light," if you will!

We know that the obedience of Mary and Joseph to God was foremost. We know that they would have embraced this information rather than question it. To question God was not in their character and, therefore, one of the very reasons they were chosen for this job over all of us. Remembering that they just received somewhat startling news, we now read further that Simeon was not finished handing out clues to the future, and one of them in particular, stung the heart of Mary with her first sorrow.

Narrowing our focus, let's review Luke 2:34 and 35 again. Fill in the blanks and hear the words in your mind, just as Mary herself must have often and mindfully replayed these carefully chosen words of Simeon.

"Behold, this child is _____ for the _____ and _____ of many

in _____, and to be a _____ that will be _____

(and _____ a sword will pierce) so that the _____ of many

_____ may be _____.

THE ANNUNCIATION

What a turn of events for Mary on this day. Was she prepared for what she was about to hear from Simeon? Let's flash back to what we know Mary to have understood up to this moment-in-time. Read Luke 1:26-35.

Wouldn't you agree that Gabriel left Mary on a "High" note, if you will? Underline or take note of every time that: God, Lord, Most High, Son of God, Holy Spirit, or Son of Most High is quoted by Gabriel in versus 28-35. What number did you get? _____ I counted that at least 7 times she was reminded that this was no ordinary visit. Gabriel had his talking points down and clearly reiterated them to Mary. There would be no mistake of whose message Gabriel was delivering.

If you had overheard this conversation, how would you have interpreted Gabriel's message?

_____

_____

_____

What differences do you see between the Annunciation message and the foretelling message delivered by Simeon?

_____

JEWISH LAW AND CUSTOMS

Mary was carefully following Jewish law and knew that she was to redeem her son and purify herself. First let's review the law of redeeming her son. See Exodus 13: 2 and 12-16. Moses was not kidding about the seriousness of this law and there is no question that Mary and Joseph would have known what was expected of them.

Who does the first-born belong to? _____

In verse 13, what happens to the animals that are not to be redeemed?

_____

Did God intend for this to be a law for this generation only? _____ Why not? What in verse 14 and again in 16 makes you believe it was to be handed down from generation to generation?

_____

_____

I love those visual words in verse 16. *Let this, then, be as a _____ on your _____ and as a _____ on your _____: with a strong hand the LORD brought us out of Egypt.* He did not say to write it on your hearts, did he? He chose two of the most exposed parts of the body. It was to be divulged for all to know, see, and follow.

Furthermore, she was to purify herself. Leviticus 12: 1-4, 6-8 gives us the detail that Mary would have known by heart. Unclean for 7 days, Day 8 is to be the circumcision of Jesus and then Mary was to wait 33 more days for her blood to purify. During this time she was not to touch anything sacred nor enter any sanctuary. At the end she was to bring her holocaust and sin offering to the priest. In turn, he would offer them up to the Lord for her atonement.

It is interesting to point out that Mary and Joseph were not, by law, required to present Jesus at the temple, however, another scripture leads us to better understand why this couple may have been led to present Jesus in this way. 1 Samuel may be the clue. Before we read it and try to piece the words into context, a little information is necessary.

Hannah was for a long time the barren one of two spouses to Elkanah. Peninnah, his other wife, had many children and would use this against Hannah through constant reproach that the Lord had left her womb childless. One day, she broke down in tears and took her troubles to the temple where she prayed humbly and earnestly to the Lord for a son. Eli, the priest, saw Hannah long at prayer and thought she was drunk. After questioning her, he realized her intentions were honorable and blessed her before she left the temple. Hannah had promised God that if he would grant her a son, she would in turn give him to the Lord. God heard her cry, and having favor upon her, blessed her with Samuel. Hannah, keeping her promise to God, dedicated her son back to Him by leaving him with Eli, the priest. Samuel would go on to do great things for God.

That leads us to the scripture. Read 1 Samuel 1:24-28.

What did Hannah take with her on her way to the temple of the Lord in Shiloh? (v24)

_____

_____

_____

Yes, Samuel was with her! After his father sacrificed the three year old bull, who approached Eli?

_____

It was clear that Eli was not expecting her, for in verse 26 she had to interrupt him or pardon herself and then explain who she was. She indicated: *...I am the woman who _____ _____, praying to the _____.*

She further explains that she prayed for the child and that her request was granted. In keeping with her promise, what did Hannah willfully and knowingly do with the son that she so desperately wanted? (v 28) _____

_____

Mary and Joseph, along with all Jews, had been praying for the Messiah. Their prayers were answered just as Hannah's had. They knew that God had shown them favor and they wanted to return the blessing to its rightful owner, God. Unlike Hannah's son, Jesus would have left with them that day but would return to the temple around age 12 to unknowingly remain in his Father's house. That day, too, would become a sorrow for Mary. Is it clearer to you why Mary would not have simply brought her offerings to the temple, but would have also felt compelled to present Jesus?

One of the neatest parts of this story is that Hannah's response and praises to God were kept intact and written upon scrolls and later into the book of 1 Samuel for others to know and pray. I believe that Mary would have known well, if not memorized, Hannah's beautiful prayer of thanksgiving. Mary also, as we do today, would have been drawn to stories that revealed God's goodness and to the character of those women before her that found favor with God. Mary would have studied them and followed their lead. Because Hannah's prayer is so beautiful a tribute to our Lord God and because we will use it later to compare some of Mary's own words, I have copied it below for us to read and absorb. Read it as if you were Mary, finding yourself with a son who indeed belongs to God. Here is the prayer taken from 1 Samuel 2:1-10.

1. "My heart exults in the LORD,
my horn is exalted in my God.
I have swallowed up my enemies;
I rejoice in my victory.
2. There is no Holy One like the LORD;
there in no Rock like our God.
3. "Speak boastfully no longer,
nor let arrogance issue from your mouths.
For an all-knowing God is the LORD,
a God who judges deeds.
4. The bows of the mighty are broken,
while the tottering gird on strength.
5. The well-fed hire themselves out for bread,
while the hungry batten on spoil.
The barren wife bears seven sons, while the mother of many languishes.
6. "The LORD puts to death and gives life;
he casts down to the nether world; he raises up again.
7. The LORD makes poor and makes rich,
he humbles, he also exalts.
8. He raises the needy from the dust;
from the ash heap he lifts up the poor,
To seat them with nobles
and make a glorious throne their heritage.
He gives to the vower his vow,
and blesses the sleep of the just.
"For the pillars of the earth are the LORD'S,

and he has set the world upon them.
9. He will guard the footsteps of his faithful ones,
but the wicked shall perish in the darkness.
For not by strength does man prevail;
10. the LORD'S foes shall be shattered.
The Most High in heaven thunders;
The LORD judges the ends of the earth,
Now may he give strength to his king, and exalt the horn of his anointed!"

I initially had trouble understanding about the horn (in the first and tenth verse) and then found that a "horn" is used to symbolize a person's strength. This made a lot more sense to me. This prayer is all about praising, honoring and fearing the Lord. Now, let's look at the Canticle of Mary in the New Testament, written over 1000 years later, as she responded to her cousin Elizabeth who was pregnant at the time with John the Baptist. Read the passage below, Luke 1:46-55.

46 "My soul proclaims the greatness of the Lord;
47 my spirit rejoices in God my savior.
48 For he has looked upon his handmaid's lowliness; behold, from now on will all ages call me blessed.
49 The Mighty One has done great things for me, and holy is his name.
50 His mercy is from age to age to those who fear him.
51 He has shown might with his arm, dispersed the arrogant of mind and heart.
52 He has thrown down the rulers from their thrones but lifted up the lowly.
53 The hungry he has filled with good things; the rich he has sent away empty.
54 He has helped Israel his servant, remembering his mercy,
55 according to his promise to our fathers, to Abraham and to his descendants forever."

As if writing a letter of thanks, Hannah and Mary passionately express their thoughts in a similar cadence. Both Hannah and Mary open their prayers by offering great homage to God. Hannah's heart exalts and her horn (strength) is exalted in her God (v1). Mary's soul proclaims and her spirit rejoices (v46-47). Both women then exclaim the greatness and holiness of God; Hannah, by stating that no one else is of His holiness or strength (Rock) (v 2) and Mary through calling him the Mighty One (v49). Our God loves for us to admire him and thank him for his blessings upon us. He loves to hear our voices in praise and these two women honor him beautifully. Do you see the similarities of the two writings? Do you agree that Mary might have absorbed some of these beliefs from centuries of custom, tradition, and writings?

Now it is your turn.

What word is repeated in Mary's verse 51 and Hannah's verse 3?

_____

Both women understand God's wrath against the arrogant, don't they?

What kinds of people do Mary (52,53) and Hannah (8) recognize as God's favored ones?

HUMILITY IS A FORM OF PREPARATION

A cleansed heart is the perfect way to begin any study. Every time we go to mass we atone for our sins and ask for forgiveness. Some of the first words spoken by the priest and by the congregation are words of humility and confession. To be cleansed with our brothers and sisters in Christ is a beautiful way to start the day and brings joy to our Lord. Furthermore, it is necessary to ready ourselves for acceptance of his Body and Blood. The following is one of the prayers we should recognize.

Catholic Link

The Catholic Mass

I confess to almighty God and to you, my brothers and sisters, that I have greatly sinned in my thoughts and in my words, in what I have done and in what I have failed to do, through my fault, through my fault, through my most grievous fault; therefore I ask blessed Mary ever-Virgin, all the Angels and Saints, and you, my brothers and sisters, to pray for me to the Lord our God.

Priest: May almighty God have mercy on us, forgive us our sins, and bring us to everlasting life.

All: Amen.

SUMMARY OF THE FIRST SORROW

If it is true that we do not learn as much in our joys as we do our sorrows, then we are in for some great teachings. These seven sorrows represent some of the deepest known to man. I hope that you have learned more about this first sorrow as we have scanned the Bible for clearer understanding and insight. I hope that when you meditate on this sorrow, that you will recall Mary's mind and heart at the time and how she so lovingly embraced this life and the sorrows that came along with it.

We can learn from Mary's actions and from her character that is revealed to us through these passages. Her strength was enormous and her focus streamlined. Think of ways that you can incorporate Mary's first sorrow into your day:

⇒ Maybe it is to praise God more often.
⇒ To realize that a pierced heart may indeed allow the thoughts of many hearts to be revealed.
⇒ Remind ourselves that we all belong to God. (even our own children)
⇒ Perhaps we will take with us a part of Mary's humility at the warning of Simeon and how she used this information to prepare herself for motherhood.
⇒ Add your own thoughts: _____

One more thought before we pray. Think about the way we react to hurtful news in our life? Do we let it bring us down or do we use it as resistance to further strengthen our own bodies and minds? Mary took Simeon's words and put them to use building her own muscle under its weight. Think of your next sorrow as a promotion. God was so pleased with your incredible form and ease at handling the current weight that he asked you to take on more.

Rejoice and leap for joy on that day! Behold, your reward will be great in heaven. Luke 6: 23

"WHERE DID YOU GET THOSE MUSCLES, BABY?"

Record some of the things that you learned about Mary through her first of seven sorrows. Include notes on her desire to imitate others who were pleasing to God and the way she handled the news from Simeon.

_____

_____

_____

_____

_____

Let's close this sorrow with the Hail Mary:

Hail Mary, full of Grace. The Lord is with you.

Blessed are you among women, and blessed is the fruit of your womb, Jesus.

Holy Mary, Mother of God, pray for us sinners, now and at the hour of our death. Amen.

The Flight Into Egypt

the second sorrow

Read Matthew 2:13-18

So many thoughts come rushing to my mind when I read these words:

⇒ The important role that the trusting servant Joseph played
⇒ The intense fear of knowing that someone of power and authority wanted to have their precious Son murdered
⇒ The nimbleness of this family to be able to leave their home and belongings at a moment's notice
⇒ The massacre of the innocent baby boys who became the first to die for our Savior, Jesus
⇒ The unfaltering prayers of our loving Mother that would have been pouring out as they left Israel in search of safety.

As we meditate on each of these thoughts, we will expand upon them and see what they have in store for us.

JOSEPH

First let's look at St. Joseph, the man of integrity and faith who still guides men as fathers and as husbands today. There is not much stated in the Bible about Joseph, yet what we do know reveals his character and obedience to God. Read Matthew 1: 18-25.

In verse 19, what kind of a man do they say Joseph is? _____

_____

_____

Being righteous is to be morally right or justifiable in your actions. Righteous people are virtuous and genuine. The moral decision to leave Mary quietly was truly justifiable and morally correct. He must have been hurt and very angry at the thought of Mary being pregnant by another. I am sure that he believed Mary to be righteous but this new discovery must have made him doubt his own judgment. He could have made a big deal out of the pregnancy and this would have been justifiable. Their community severely punished, and sometimes stoned such women to their death. This, also, would have been justifiable, as he could have believed it his duty to call attention to her and keep his name clear of wrongdoing. Who wouldn't believe this righteous man?

Remaining on verse 19, it states: "*...since he was a righteous man, yet* _____ *to expose her to shame,* _____ *to divorce her quietly.*" We learn much more about Joseph in this sentence when we read it carefully. First, he was "unwilling" to expose her. Unwilling means that he did not vindictively decide to judge her, he did not follow custom or law for just punishment, nor did he say that he really *didn't want to* expose her, but wouldn't be upset if somehow it slipped out. No, the author was very clear that he was <u>unwilling</u> to take that approach, keeping with his virtuous reputation. We also see that it was HE who "decided" to divorce her in quiet. He was a decisive man and did not seek every other person he knew to help him decide what to do. HE chose what to do, HE was unwilling to expose her, and HE kept it a secret! All before knowing that this had anything to do with God. This act, therefore, was not out of obedience; it was the act of a righteous man. God and Mary chose well.

Joseph had proven himself worthy to be head of this most holy household and so it was he who received the warning message to flee to Egypt and again to return after Herod's death. Way to go Joseph!

KING HEROD

Now let's look at how devastating the news, of wanting to destroy their son, truly was to this young couple. By now they know that they have been asked to parent and protect no ordinary child of God. This is our Savior, the only true begotten Son of God and someone wants him dead. Not unlike today, there is enormous greed, insecurity, and evil that lurks among our communities. The problem with this news was that the paranoid, evil, and greedy person flexing his muscle against the infant Jesus had immense power and authority. We cannot imagine this power in our own country, as in most of our cities and towns across the U.S. we have checks and balances built in for evil people in high places. However, a crooked king could make an edict with no questions asked and this, we know from the historian Josephus (who knew, followed and wrote about King Herod), was totally in character for this violent ruler. The soldiers would stop at nothing to fulfill their king's order.

Reflecting on these two men, Joseph and King Herod, record some of their character differences.

_____

_____

_____

God blessed both men with decisiveness and authority, yet there is a vast contrast between their practices of these skills. Why do you think that one powerful man chose evil ways to defend his personal kingdom while the other chose righteous ways to build up God's kingdom? (Do you ever wonder if your decisions are serving the right kingdom?)

_____

_____

_____

THE HOLY AND NIMBLE FAMILY

OK, I hear you, God! I admit it! This is a lesson I am still struggling with, all right? Being nimble or simple enough to drop everything is not easy for me. Being nimble helped Mary react to this call, but I must also add that no part of this sorrow had to do with what material things Mary had to leave behind. She was prepared to deal with whatever God asked her to do because she led her life in that way. I am a pack rat for things and I do love my safe and warm home. Now if I received a warning that my children were in danger, yes-absolutely, I would leave everything behind in an instant. Could I do it with the ease and grace that our Holy Family did? Nope! Without complaints? No way!

In what ways are you nimble and simple? _____

_____

_____

How can we simplify our lives so that the clutter of it does not weigh us down? How can we teach our children that less is better in a world that thrives on abundance? How can we better clarify the blurry line between what we need and what we want? How about the things we need to want? Need to want means that I don't need it as a necessity, but it sure does come in handy or it sure does allow me to help others in some way. Girl Scout cookies come to mind! Let's face it, most of us have more than we need to live, but the economy needs people to consume things, right?

In what areas do you wish you could improve, simplify, or become more nimble?

_____

_____

I will never forget the death and subsequent funeral of my husband's Aunt DeDe, or Sister Delia as the Providence Nuns and others called her. Committed to her vow of Poverty, her possessions at death included enough things to fill only two shallow drawers and a small bureau that held a sweater, bathrobe, and a few shirts and skirts. At the very instant that the ushers closed her casket, the earth quaked across central Indiana, which was an extremely rare but timely occurrence. We all looked around in utter amazement with perhaps a tiny bit of apprehension. I could only think how Jesus loves bringing his brides home. He reminded me that His love is bigger, greater, and more powerful than anything here on Earth. Sister Delia Leonard knew that and the rattling message at her funeral was a profound wake-up call for me.

MARY PRAYS FOR THE INNOCENT BOYS' LIVES

We stated earlier that Josephus was a historian who followed Herod the Great. Many scholars find it interesting that Josephus did not even mention this slaughter in his writing. The only evidence of it is found in Matthew, as it was probably insignificant when compared to the other heinous acts of this king. I can assure you that it was not insignificant to the estimated seven to twenty infant boys' mothers who lost their sons that day, and it was not insignificant to our Blessed Mother, Mary.

Mary was no doubt friendly with the other Jewish mothers who had sons the age of Jesus. She would have seen them at Temple, in the marketplace, or knew them as good friends and neighbors. Bethlehem was a small village, estimated in the days of our Lord to have the population of only 300 to 1000 people. They would have known these fellow Jews and probably prayed with them or for them daily.

This massacre would have caused Mary to weep and to pray both a thanksgiving for her son's safety and a prayer for the souls of the boys she could most likely mention by name. Also, she would pray for strength and understanding for the mothers and fathers that she also would have known by name. Almost unbelievable, Mary would have also prayed for Herod. She would have prayed for his heart to soften and for his anxieties and paranoia to heal, knowing that others in time would fall to his anger, jealousy, and greed. She would have fought for the very soul who tried to destroy her son, until she could fight no more.

This reminds me of another holy women who spoke the following discerning words because sometimes we fall short of following Mary's perfect example. *"If you judge people, you have no time to love them." Mother Teresa*

Is there anyone that we should be praying for rather than scoffing, criticizing, or fearing? Wouldn't that soul, with their seemingly endless energy and determination, be better on our team if they could turn it around to honor Jesus? Saul, the strong-willed and devout Jew who consented to Stephen's execution (Acts 8:1), persecuted many Christians (Acts 8 and 9), and asked to lead a group to destroy the apostles, is one such man. After hearing the voice of Jesus on the way to Damascus, his eyes were opened to His Savior and he became one of the strongest voices for conversion. His old friends became his enemies and tormented him, however, Saul used their tormenting to fuel the fire for Christ within him ... *But Saul grew all the stronger and confounded the Jews who lived in Damascus, proving that this is the Messiah. Acts 9:22*

Do you know a Saul? Without using a name, write a prayer of thanksgiving for the converted "Saul" you may know *or* a heartfelt prayer for the "Saul" of this world who has yet to hear God's call?

_____

_____

_____

_____

_____

MARY CONTINUES TO PRAY FOR THE LIVES OF THE INNOCENT

I cannot leave this sorrow before I share with you a parallel that so tugs at my heart when I breathe in and contemplate the massacre of the innocent. All of us, of this generation, carry the burden of a grave sin upon our backs. We still slaughter the innocent through abortion. We allow for the demoralization of women by letting society tell us that a baby is dispensable. What about the poor souls who were forced or frightened into the "sweep it under the carpet" promise, only to find out that it was like pulling a rug over an elephant?

God gave this miracle of bringing forth life to women alone. This blessing from God is not to be taken lightly. You would think that women would treasure and protect, at any cost, this invaluable and precious gift. It is only a woman whose intricacies can begin and sustain life; life of a human, consecrated by God, that has never been before and will never be again. How can we live in a world that attacks the innocent and calls it a choice? How can we disregard the preferential treatment women have received from God and judge its gifts as bad timing? How do we dare question the human creation God consecrates through His love and care? Herod's slaughter was a **choice** he made from **insecurities** and **greed**. Does it sound familiar?

The Catholic Church has strongly disagreed with and condemned the act of abortion. They speak out against its legality and have remained steadfast as this highly controversial issue continues to be debated in America. Their voice, although unwavering against abortion, warmly extends consolation for those who need God's forgiveness. They have funded and instituted many educational programs to help counter the proliferation of this grave contradiction to moral law.

Catholic Link

Catechism of the Catholic Church

2258 "Human life is sacred because from its beginning it involves the creative action of God and it remains for ever in a special relationship with the Creator, who is its sole end.

2270 Human life must be respected and protected absolutely from the moment of conception. From the first moment of his existence, a human being must be recognized as having the rights of a person-among which is the inviolable right of every innocent being to life.

Before I formed you in the womb I knew you, and before you were born I consecrated you.

My frame was not hidden from you, when I was being made in secret, intricately wrought in the depths of the earth.

2271 Since the first century the Church has affirmed the moral evil of every procured abortion. This teaching has not changed and remains unchangeable. Direct abortion, that is to say, abortion willed either as an end or a means, is gravely contrary to the moral law:

You shall not kill the embryo by abortion and shall not cause the newborn to perish.
 God, the Lord of life, has entrusted to men the noble mission of safeguarding life, and men must carry it out in a manner worthy of themselves. Life must be protected with the utmost care from the moment of conception: abortion and infanticide are abominable crimes.

Did you find any surprises in the Catholic Link? _____ What do you think is most important to remember?

_____

_____

_____

Just to put it in perspective, during the Holocaust, it is estimated that between 9 million and 11 million people, including the estimated 6 million European Jews, fell victim to Adolf Hitler's greed and destruction. This annihilation and devastation on innocent lives was vowed by many to never be repeated; yet from 1973 through 2006, over 37 million legal abortions have been performed in the United States alone. This tragedy more than triples the deaths attributed to the Holocaust. These statistics are according to Centers for Disease Control and Prevention (CDC) whose numbers are comparatively conservative to other studies since they record only those areas or states who voluntarily offer their data. The web addresses for this information were found in November of 2009 at: http://www.cdc.gov/reproductivehealth/Data_Stats/Abortion.htm and http://www.cdc.gov/mmwr/preview/mmwrhtml/ss5212a1.htm#fig1. During the 21 years from 1977 through 1997, there were over one million abortions each year. In fact, the sad total for this time span is a staggering 27,170,295 innocent lives. These statistics are not widely publicized, however this is a huge part of American life, or should I say death. The Catholic Church has one of the strongest voices against abortion. I am proud to be associated with their steadfast and unwavering conviction, but I also know that their voice is amplified and given new life through our individual and united voices. Ask Mary to help us be heard as we defend God's most innocent children.

SUMMARY OF THE SECOND SORROW

This second sorrow holds many lessons and much sadness. It is difficult to fully comprehend the immense disaster and destruction that can be wrought from greed, paranoia, insecurity, and evil. Herod and Joseph had the power to effect change and so do we. Our culture is a product of the evils and righteousness that preceded us, and what we leave behind will set the stage for future generations. The ripple effect lasts long after the initial act, leaving others to swim in the either calm or treacherous waters we created.

Let us pray for those who persecute and ask that God either soften their heart for His glory or strengthen our armor against them. Let us pray that our actions build up rather than tear down, calm rather than trouble, encourage rather than paralyze. Let us find compassion in our will to serve. Let us be reminded that righteousness and integrity comes from years of consistent behavior and not from a fleeting moment of prayer. May we always encourage each other to be righteous people of virtue and ask God to trust us with more!

I ask the Lord to help me clear out the junk so I can focus on hearing His call.

What is your prayer?

_____

_____

_____

Record some of the things you learned about Mary in this sorrow. You may want to include things about the way she chose to live her life, the sacrifice that would bring her sorrow, and the way she would, and still does pray for every soul.

_____

_____

_____

As we allow this sorrow of massacre on the innocent lives to settle in, let us pray:

Hail Mary, full of Grace. The Lord is with you.

Blessed are you among women, and blessed is the fruit of your womb, Jesus.

Holy Mary, Mother of God, pray for us sinners, now and at the hour of our death. Amen.

The Loss of the
Child Jesus in the Temple

the third sorrow

JESUS FOUND

Read Luke 2: 41-52

Have you ever had a misunderstanding? One where you believed that you had made your point perfectly clear or had trusted that you understood another's intentions only to find out that great anxieties arose within the other party or you over a miscommunication? Sometimes hours go by and sometimes nearly an entire lifetime before the final missing clue fits into place and the misunderstanding dissolves before our very eyes. Deep in my heart I have come to realize that this was no ordinary mishap. A deeper lesson for all of us lies underneath the pain and anxiety of Mary and Joseph as they sought their son and Lord. Let's see where our hearts take us as we meditate this anxious-driven, heart-throbbing sorrow.

To fully understand this sorrow we must first visualize the feast of Passover, the journey to Jerusalem, and the festival custom that would have been very familiar to the writer, Luke, to much of his audience during this time, but not so familiar to our generation. Jewish custom, according to Deuteronomy 16: 16, tells us:

"Three times a year, then, every male among you shall appear before the LORD,
your God, in the place which he chooses: at the feast of Unleavened Bread,
at the feast of Weeks, and at the feast of Booths."

These festivals, handed down by God to the Jewish people, became significant landmarks in the New Testament with Jesus providing the bridge to the New Covenant and the gateway into the great festival we will share in Heaven.

Even on Earth, we receive glimpses of what this festival in heaven may be like. Every time I am allowed to understand with more clarity a scripture by reading someone's insightful thoughts, hearing a priest or speaker untangle the words for me, or simply hearing the whisper of God while I read His book, I am enlightened and changed forever. The deeper I go into His Word, the more I see how much He loves us, has always loved us, and will love us for eternity. It is not simply "how much" he loves us (quantity), but more importantly "how" he shows us "much" love (quality) that will keep us mesmerized.

His perfect and endless love is all so clear for a moment and then like a glass of water, is emptied back into a seemingly bottomless well. I love those days in which I can sit with my glass of water and marvel at its clarity; drinking in as much as I can before the glass spills out its leftover contents, feeding the reservoir inside me. The deepness and darkness of the well sometimes makes me wonder if I will ever get to taste that refreshment again, and then I remember that the well serves me, as my holding tank of spiritual thoughts and God moments. I can, and will need to many times during my life, drop my empty pail into the well of memories nearly forgotten, and bring forth the sustenance needed. Our minds cannot ingest the great wonder of our Lord. Only by droplets, sips, and gulps, do we take in the mystery of His greatness and His master plan that has always thoughtfully and intentionally included you and me.

God's attentive timing and infinite wisdom translate to gifts of hope and lessons of faith to us, his followers. Let's try now to piece together the feasts to determine why, out of the three journeys to Jerusalem, God chose the Passover feast as the one to retain his Son.

Read Exodus 23:14-17 for a brief highlight of the three feasts.

First feast is:_____

What must they eat for seven days? _____

What was this month called? _____

What was the significance of this month? _____

The second feast is: _____

What were they to bring? _____

_____

The third feast is: _____

What end-of-year job would indicate that it was time for this feast? _____

_____

It is important to note the timing of these feasts. The first would have occurred in the springtime (March or April). The second would be in early summer (May or June) and the third would be early fall (September or October). God retained Jesus after the first feast. Let's study the parallels and find the threads that have been woven for us from the Old Testament to the New Testament about each feast. We have some work ahead of us but the journey back and forth is worth the time.

FEAST OF UNLEAVENED BREAD (the first feast)

Begin by reading only the Old Covenant descriptions for the first feast. (Put your hand over the New Covenant answers if it helps.) See if these thoughts bring to mind any familiar New Covenant scripture passages or stories. Then begin to picture in your mind why this feast was so important to God and Jesus. When you are done guessing, read the New Covenant replies and then the descriptions for each point.

Feast of Unleavened Bread

OLD COVENANT	NEW COVENANT
1. First day of feast is Passover	1. Last Supper was Passover meal
2. Feast of Unleavened bread follows on next day	2. Jesus' crucifixion was next day
3. God's people saved from slavery in Egypt	3. God's people saved from slavery of sin
4. Month of Abib- "ripe grain"	4. Jesus had completed his mission on Earth
5. Springtime feast - March or April	5. The Resurrection and Easter Holiday
6. "Bread of Affliction"- no corruption	6. Jesus' body did not succumb to corruption
7. Sheaf of first fruits waved for acceptance	7. God's "first fruit" (Jesus) made us acceptable
8. Sacred veil in sanctuary symbolized wall between God and man	8. Veil is torn and opened as Jesus ends the wall keeping us from God
9. Holocaust of an unblemished lamb	9. Sacrifice of the sinless Christ (Lamb of God)
10. Libation of wine poured out to honor God	10. Jesus' blood shed to honor God on our behalf. God's love poured out through the Holy Spirit
Significance: Bread, Wine, and Sacrifice offered by his people to make themselves acceptable to God	Significance: Body, Blood, and Sacrifice offered by God to perfectly redeem his people

27

Please note: Each point above will be explained in the corresponding text below. A complete listing of Scripture passages can be found at the end of each point.

JESUS IS OUR PASSOVER PROMISE

Feast of the Passover and feast of the Unleavened Bread - Of the three annual feasts that the Jewish Pilgrims would have been required to travel to Jerusalem, God chose to retain His Son on this occasion. Was it by chance or did it, like everything else God does, have a significant purpose to His overall plan? It has always bothered me, too, why God chose to separate Jesus from His parents instead of just communicating it directly to them through an angel or perhaps a warning in another dream. Was it an oversight on God's part? No, not at all. It, instead, is for us to discover and to learn from; for this was the feast that thrust another arrow directly into the heart of our Sweet Lady.

1. First day of feast is Passover – Last Supper was Passover meal. Leviticus 23:4-5 defines the proper time of the Passover. The sacred assembly was to begin at evening twilight on day fourteen of the first month. In the first Passover, the believers used the blood of an unblemished lamb to cover the doorway so that their firstborn would be passed over by the plague of death and that they may then be led to freedom from slavery. The New Covenant believers will use the blood of God's unblemished firstborn Jesus to cover our sins that the plague of eternal death may pass over us and lead us to freedom through Christ. Therefore, upon our death, we will experience the fullness of the Passover Sacrifice. (See the Catholic Link below and pay special attention to what Catholics call Christian Funerals!) The Last Supper meal, where Jesus revealed the New Covenant promises, was indeed this very feast; the feast the apostles were to prepare the upper room for was the Passover meal. (Lv 23:4-5, Luke 22:7)

Catholic Link

Catechism of the Catholic Church

ARTICLE 2, CHRISTIAN FUNERALS

1680

All the sacraments, and principally those of Christian initiation, have as their goal the last Passover of the child of God which, through death, leads him into the life of the Kingdom. Then what he confessed in faith and hope will be fulfilled: "I look for the resurrection of the dead, and the life of the world to come.

The Christian's Last Passover

1681

The Christian meaning of death is revealed in the light of the Paschal mystery of the death and resurrection of Christ in whom resides our only hope. The Christian who dies in Christ Jesus is "away from the body and at home with the Lord."

---

2. Feast of unleavened bread follows on next day – Jesus' crucifixion was next day. Leviticus further states that day fifteen of this month is the Lord's Feast of Unleavened Bread. This means that Jesus' death by Crucifixion would have occurred on the first day of the Feast of Unleavened Bread. The original focal point of the feast, the unleavened bread, was transformed into the Body of Christ upon the cross, who is remembered now through the consecrated host, or unleavened bread. *Therefore let us celebrate the feast, not with the old yeast, the yeast of malice and wickedness, but with the unleavened bread of sincerity and truth. 1 Corinthians 5:8.* (Lv. 23:6, Luke 23:24, 1 Corinthians 5:8)

3. God's people saved from slavery in Egypt – God's people saved from slavery of sin by Christ's death. Exodus 23:15 states that this feast was to be an annual reminder that the Lord brought them out of Egypt, saving them from slavery. Upon Jesus' crucifixion, we were saved from our slavery to sin. We also continue this tradition through Holy Week, Good Friday, and Easter and pass our faith to our children through these days of reflection and feast. (Exodus 23:15, Romans 5:8-11)

4. Month of Abib is "ripe grain" – Jesus had completed his mission on Earth. Deuteronomy explains that the month of Passover is the month of Abib. Translated, Abib means, "ear of grain" or "ripe grain." (This corresponds to our springtime, March and April.) This "ripe grain" correlates to Jesus' mission on earth being fulfilled or "ripe" and the passing from one covenant to the other. (Dt. 16:1, Exodus 23:15, John 17:4)

5. Springtime feast is March or April – The Resurrection and Easter holiday. As stated above, this feast was celebrated in springtime. The Resurrection of Christ was therefore in springtime, and provides us with hope for our own resurrection to eternal life with God in Heaven. Springtime represents new life with the budding of trees and plants. Our Easter holiday is a joyful representation of the Feast of Unleavened Bread where we annually remember Jesus' sacrifice during Lent, and especially Holy Week, as we prepare ourselves anew for Christ's Resurrection (Dt. 16:1, Luke 24: 5-6).

6. Bread of affliction with no corruption – Jesus' body did not succumb to corruption. Neither the unleavened bread nor the body of Jesus would succumb to corruption, but be preserved. God instructed the Israelites to make unleavened bread so that they could flee Egypt rapidly when given instruction to do so. Leavened bread will mold; unleavened bread, more like a cracker, will be preserved and allow them nourishment for the desert journey. Dt. 16: 3 tells us that unleavened bread is also to be remembered by the Israelites as the "bread of affliction" so that they, for all days, remember that in frightened haste they departed Egypt and the shackles of slavery. Jesus is our "bread of affliction" where his great suffering paid for our sins and ended the bondage of our slavery to sin. In John 20:27 the "doubting Thomas" saw the miracle of Jesus' uncorrupted body for himself as the resurrected Jesus instructed him to place his finger upon his hand and place his hand into his side. Jesus had to prove his resurrection to Thomas so that he would believe. Jesus added, *"blessed are those who have not seen and have believed."* We, too, must always remember Jesus' sacrifice and it is our duty to pass it down to future generations. (Dt. 16:3, John 20:27, 1 Timothy 1:17)

7. Sheaf of first fruits waved for acceptance – God's first fruit (Jesus) made us acceptable. Leviticus 23:10-11 tells us that God's instructions to Moses stated that upon reaping their harvests, they must bring a sheaf of the first fruits to the priest. The waving of the sheaf of first fruits by the priest would cleanse or "make acceptable" the person who offered the sheaf to the Lord. God sent Jesus, His and Mary's first fruit, to make us acceptable to God. Remember: ...and blessed is the "fruit" of your womb, Jesus. Without Jesus we are not worthy, but through Jesus we are purified.

8. Sacred veil in sanctuary symbolized wall between God and man – Veil is torn and opened as Jesus ends the wall keeping us from God. According to Mark 15: 38, upon Jesus' death, the veil of the Temple sanctuary was torn in two from top to bottom. To understand this significance we must first understand the importance of the veil. The veil represented the wall between God and man. Gathered from several books of the Old Testament, we know that the veil was set before the inner most part of the sanctuary (also called the Holy of holies). To show the reverence to God, no man was allowed to enter beyond this veil. The only exception was the priest, who was allowed to enter only once a year on Yom Kippur, the Day of Atonement. Acknowledging that Jesus was the One and only Messiah that ended the separation of man to God, this occurrence (of a split veil) as Jesus breathed his last earthly breath, forever fulfilled our first fruit offering thus making us forever acceptable to God. Our sins had been nailed to the cross with our Savior, and we received everlasting atonement. (Exodus 36:35-38, 38:18, 40:33, 26:33 Hebrews 6:19-20 and 9:3-12, 24-27)

UNDERSTANDING GOD'S LIMITS: Read Leviticus 10: 1-2. What happened to Aaron's two sons who did not keep sacred the fire of the Lord's presence?

_____

_____

Read Leviticus 16:1-2. What instructions did the Lord God have for Aaron in regards to entering the sanctuary, inside the veil?

_____

_____

In Hebrews 6:19-20 who entered the interior sanctuary behind the veil?

_____ On whose behalf did Jesus enter? _____

Verse 19 calls Jesus the "anchor of our soul." What do you think this means?

_____

_____

9. Holocaust of an unblemished lamb – sacrifice of the sinless Christ (Lamb of God) Leviticus 23: 12 says: *On this day, when your sheaf is waved, you shall offer to the LORD for a holocaust an unblemished yearling lamb.* This unblemished lamb would be sacrificed (or slaughtered) to fulfill the requirements for acceptability. John 1:29 tells us that John

the Baptist referred to Jesus as *"The Lamb of God who takes away the sin of the world."* Our Catholic liturgy uses these exact words just before Holy Communion during the Breaking of the Bread. The Consecrated Bread has become the Body of Jesus and we are embarking on physically and spiritually accepting the very Body of the Lamb that was sacrificed for our Salvation. "Unblemished" in the Old Testament and "without blemish" or sinless in the New Testament. Leviticus 23:12, John 1:29)

10. Libation of wine poured out to honor God – Jesus' blood shed to honor God on our behalf and God's love poured out to us through the Holy Spirit. A libation is a drink "poured out" to honor Deity, Creator, God. The term libation was not used lightly and did not refer to any drink that was poured for consuming. This word was reserved for God and was used during ceremonies to honor their Creator. Jesus fulfilled this "pouring out" by shedding his blood upon the cross, pouring out water and blood as the lance struck his side, and by establishing the cup of the new covenant where ordinary wine becomes for us the blood of Christ. Romans 5:5 adds; *...because the love of God has been poured out into our hearts through the holy Spirit that has been given to us.* It is all linked. The blood of the lamb was sacrificed to honor God and to ask for his acceptance. The blood of Jesus was sacrificed to honor God and to permanently cover the sin that makes us unacceptable to God. God holds back nothing from his children and His love spills over us with the Holy Spirit. I find it amazing and heart warming that God chose to honor us in a similar way to His own request for honor, albeit much more grand, divine and superior to our attempts at atonement. (Leviticus 23:13, John 19:34, Luke 22:20, Romans 5:5)

I hope that you learned as much as I did from studying this feast. My mind is boggled with His attention to every detail and I know that there are many more correlations that could be derived. You may have already known these fulfilled prophesies from Old Testament to New Testament, but I hope this exercise provided you with some food-for-thought. You might want to add some of your own favorite scripture passages to these covenants that more profoundly speak to you about this feast and the significance it has on our lives as Christians.

HARVESTING OF GRAIN AND MEN

The Second Festival- Feast of the Grain Harvest, (aka, Feast of Weeks and Pentecost)

The Old Covenant's first feast was a foreshadowing of our New Covenant through Jesus Christ our Savior. The ultimate sacrifice and obedience of Jesus' death upon a cross forever fulfilled the required acceptance this feast provided. A curious mind might suspect that if this feast held such significance then also must the remaining two feasts. I believe that to be true. Let's first try to find our answers within scripture and then I will summarize the feast at the end of this portion. Read Deuteronomy 16:9-12 for some key information. In verse 10, what is the proportion measurement for the freewill offering? _____

_____

God commands them to make merry but dictates who they are to include. Write each of the names mentioned in verse 11. _____

_____

Later known as Pentecost, this feast has significance in the Old Testament as the celebration of God's blessings, which occurred seven "weeks" or "fifty" (Pente is Greek for fifty) days from the feast of First Fruits/Unleavened Bread. It was to be calculated from the day when the sickle, or harvesting tool, is first used on the grain. This would be equivalent to our early summer (May to June).

The New Testament fulfills this feast under the New Covenant at the conclusion of Pentecost. Read **Acts 2:1-8**. In verse 1, it states that they were all in one place to celebrate what feast? _____ _____ God waited until Pentecost had been fulfilled or completed before sending the Holy Spirit, the blessing to live inside us. This would be the last time that Pentecost would be looked at the same as in the Old Testament for the Holy Spirit would pour into this house and into the very being of these men to "fill" them with so much more. In verse 2, the noise _____ the entire house in which they were. In verse 4, they were all _____with the Holy Spirit. You may wonder why I wanted you to write out the word "filled" twice. It is because this word so perfectly describes how they felt on that day. Perhaps it was because they felt its presence, or they were overwhelmed by its sensation. Maybe it was like us being filled with joy. Whatever it was, these statements clarify for us that it was not a mere thought or suggestion. Something happened to them and they all felt it, thus they too were "filled."

Also, isn't it fitting that God foreshadowed His call to all people through the Feast of Weeks, in which you already wrote above who was to attend the feast. In all of His wisdom, he used this feast, where son, daughter, Levite, and slave were accustomed to gather so that He could properly demonstrate the power of the Spirit. Who was represented at this feast? (verse 5)

_____

Yet how did they each hear them speak? (verse 6) _____

By the end of this glorious day a new kind of harvest would take place. God, in keeping with the timing and significance of the feast, brings forth a new harvest. Forward to the end of Acts 2, specifically verses 41 and 47. What did having the Holy Spirit allow the apostles to harvest for God's kingdom? _____ Grapes _____ 3,000 persons plus adding every day _____ Fish

Isn't it amazing how God works and isn't it incredible that the same Spirit that "filled" the Apostles still "fills" us today and the strength is no less from the wear. We can do great things with God!

Record anything special that you would like to remember about the feast of Pentecost.

_____

_____

_____

Here is the summary of what you have uncovered through scripture for the second feast:

Feast of Grain Harvest

aka. Feast of Weeks and Pentecost

OLD COVENANT	NEW COVENANT
1. 50 days after Feast of Unleavened Bread	1. Jesus' Resurrection to Ascension
2. Harvesting grain sustains life	2. Holy Spirit sustains God's message
3. Offering required is to be equal to your blessings	3. Each required to give according to their blessings
4. All inclusive gathering	4. Everyone is called
5. Early Summer harvest was brought to God as an offering and prayer for the bountiful crops to come	5. The first Pentecost with the Holy Spirit harvested 3000 men to begin and rapidly spread Christianity
Significance: First harvest used to sustain life and honor God. Freewill offering in proportion to blessings.	Significance: The Holy Spirit sent to sustain life and honor God. Freewill offering in proportion to blessings. (Some things never change!)

A FORETELLING OF HEAVEN (the third feast)

(Making it into the barn!)

Feast of the Fruit Harvest (aka the Feast of Booths)- I would like for all of you to come along with me on a little discovery journey. While working on this study, many things came to mind. Some of which are included on these pages and some still buried in my notes. This is one idea I will share with you to see if you come to the same conclusion about the significance of the Feast of Booths.

The NAB notes for Lv23: 24 states that this was a joyful observance of the vintage and fruit harvest. It continues, by describing in Lv 23:42, that for seven days the Israelites would remember their journey through the desert by camping on streets or on rooftops in "booths" made of branches. They were to remember that God led their ancestors from Egypt and they were wanderers in the desert. Dwellings of handmade "booths" (temporary structures used for shelter) were their only homes. This feast occurred on the 15th day of the seventh month, which we know would equate to sometime in September or October, according to the correlation to the feasts. Lv 23:23 states that New Year's Day was to be kept on the 1st day of the seventh month so this feast was to be only 14 days later. Again, all people were to enjoy this feast including, family, slave, alien, orphan and widow. Read Deuteronomy 16:13-14 with me, *"You shall celebrate the feast of Booths for seven days, when you have gathered in the produce from your threshing floor and wine press. You shall make merry at your feast..."* In Dt 16:16-17 it also states: *"No one shall appear before the LORD empty-handed, but each of you with as much as he can give, in proportion to the blessings which the LORD, your God, has bestowed on you.*

These passages sounded so familiar so I began researching to find where I had just read about the threshing floor in the New Testament. Behold, it is found in Matthew 3:10-12 and it follows closely to the words of the feast although it is talking about Jesus as the one who will come to harvest his goods. Let's read it now. What happens to the trees that do not bear fruit (compare to coming empty handed to the feast)? _____

_____

_____

What are Jesus' intentions for those, like wheat, who will remain on the threshing floor?

_____

(Compare to the produce and wine gathered into the barn before the feast). What are His intentions for those that can be easily separated from the harvested goods? _____

_____ (Compare to the discarded chaff that would have been burned before the feast). In case this sounds confusing to you, I will give you my limited farming expertise! The stalks, when shaken down, will allow the good grains of wheat to fall to the floor and the chaff will lie on top. A winnowing fan will easily separate the good from the bad forcing the light-weighted chaff to be blown away and leaving the wheat (with substance or weight) to remain on the threshing floor. As the chaff is cleared away for burning, the wheat is gathered into the barn.

There was also the significance of the wheat and the wine that rang a familiar bell. Why only mention wheat and wine when other produce was harvested at the same time? Could it be because this festival of sorts depicts for us the Judgment Day when Jesus, our bread (made of wheat) and wine comes in all His glory to gather His wheat (us) into His barn (heaven) while casting the chaff (evil) into the unquenchable fire. If this is to be a foretelling of the feast at the end of times, you may want to look to see what else God may have in store for us.

Lv. 23:36 states:

"On that solemn closing you shall do no sort of work"

Dt. 16:15 says,

"For seven days you shall celebrate this pilgrim feast in honor of the Lord, your God,
in the place he chooses; since the Lord, your God, has blessed you in all your crops
and in all your undertakings, you shall do naught but make merry."

Let's review: (Lv. from above) God wants us to: *"do no* _____ ___ _____.*"*
(Dt. from above) states that we are to celebrate that we have been blessed: *"in all your crops*
and in all your _____ *, you shall do* _____ *but make*

_____ *.*

I can't wait to see the feast in Heaven where we bow before our God, giving Him great honor forever more, and celebrate our blessings with the very One who has blessed us. Furthermore, I am all-in for doing naught and making merry! How about you?

Another visual summary for you to ponder:

Fruit Harvest

aka. Feast of Booths

OLD COVENANT	NEW COVENANT
1. End of year harvest- early Fall	1. End of times harvest of men
2. Bring produce from fields	2. Bringing us all in for Judgment
3. Joyful observance of vintage and fruit harvest	3. Joyful observance of Jesus' fruit-bearing followers
4. To remember wandering through the desert	4. Wandering Earth before being called home
5. Handmade or temporary booths	5. Our temporary housing on Earth
6. No one shall come to the Lord empty-handed	6. Everyone is called, some will not be prepared
7. Celebration of the produce from threshing floor and wine press	7. Jesus will gather the grain (his people) into the barn and the discarded will be burned
Significance: This celebration was twofold: Thanksgiving for the gathered produce and for special blessings for future crops	*Significance: This celebration shall be twofold: Thanksgiving for our days on Earth and special blessings for our eternal dwelling*

MARY'S FAITH

Awesome! We have made it through the tough part. Now let's use what we have learned to help identify with this sorrow. Reopen the Bible to Luke 2: 41-52 and let's read it again with our new insight and understanding.

We know that God chose this feast to retain his son, Jesus, because HE WAS the Passover lamb. (verse 41). His crucifixion and rising from the dead would complete the Passover promise of true freedom through Christ. Jesus was to be the sacrificial lamb of the New Covenant and Jesus' last Passover meal would also be known as the Last Supper. Jesus would have understood all of this and may have even gone to the festival knowing that he must stay to honor his Father. (verse 49). Many of the holiest people and great philosophers would have also traveled to Jerusalem for this feast and he would be able to hone the mastery of his earthly mission by conversing with them, for it was not time yet for his powers to be revealed. (verse 46-47). Jesus also would have used these three days to pray to and receive any additional instruction from God, his Father. (verse 52).

Mary and Joseph loved Jesus very much and would never have left him alone if God had not handled it in this way. They would never have left Jerusalem if they understood that God wanted to retain him and if they had stayed to guard him for these three days, Jesus would not have been able to completely put his dependence on God. Remember that not long before this, Mary and Joseph were fleeing the country to save their son from certain termination! Do you really think they would have allowed him the "alone" time needed to complete this work? (verse 48). Do you think that God planted a little detour or distraction for the holy couple to allow him unobstructed time with His son? (verse 50). What are your thoughts? _____

_____

_____

Now let's spend a little time on the one line that caused me to stop in my tracks. Finish the verse here and then we will talk about it. It is in verse 51. *"He went down with them and came to Nazareth, and was obedient to them;* _____

_____

_____."

Let me play out a couple other scenarios for you as I think of my own possible replies. Perhaps something like, "his mother, being furious at his lack of concern and respect for them, continued to remind him of it every time they left the house." How about this one? "His mother cried and wailed for days over the thought of nearly losing him." Or this, "His mother, wanting to prove her innocence, told everyone what had happened so she did not look like a fool." Read again what you just wrote above. What a response to a God and a son who had just put her through the wringer. What faith, what patience, and what humility she had to simply stow these things in her heart. Answer this for me. Many relatives and acquaintances knew that Mary and Joseph had lost Jesus and that they had left the caravan to find him. Having studied this amazing woman, what do you think was Mary's response to the inevitable question, "Oh Mary, you found Jesus. What happened?"

_____

_____

_____

_____

As I mediate on this sorrow, I cannot seem to shake a frightening thought. The anxiety wrought in three days of searching would, by all counts, pale in comparison to the unsettled desperation and fear that would relentlessly rip at their hearts each of the three nights. Why does darkness allow our minds to go places that daylight will not? Why do fears turn to monsters as wake turns to slumber? How can everyone else sleep while a child is missing from his parents? These would have been the killer hours, when both anxiety and exhaustion would be at their peak. Joseph and Mary would have endured much before finding him safe within the Temple.

Job 7:4 If in bed I say, "When shall I arise?" then the night drags on;
I am filled with restlessness until the dawn.

LISTENING FOR OUR CALL

Jesus was called to stay in Jerusalem. Has God ever called you to do something that may seem out of the ordinary for your character? Maybe it was to say something to a complete stranger or to do an act of kindness that you would not have thought of on your own yet strongly felt compelled to do? Sometimes we are called to venture outside our safety net and well past the assumed societal boundaries to find our God and the will he has for us.

Saints often are called to a life "out of the ordinary." Mother Teresa first felt God's call at age 12 and left the comforts of her home at the age of 18 to join the Sisters of Loreto. Her parents had great faith themselves, yet I doubt that their hopes and dreams for their daughter ever included the danger, sickness, and extreme poverty she would be called to seek and serve in Calcutta, India. Yet, we now know, that it was God's dream and, because Agnes Gonxha Bojaxhiu (Mother Teresa) said yes to the Almighty call, it was accomplished in spectacular fashion. God calls each of us in different ways to be his saints.

What calls have you answered yes to? _____

_____

_____

What calls do you fear might be considered unanswered? _____

_____

_____

If you wrote anything in the unanswered section, pray about it. If you did not, are you alive? Hello? Every one of us who breathes has a call and even the saints had lists of things that they wanted to get around to but didn't have time to finish. We should all be lucky enough to breathe our last still aching to do more for God. So now back to the list. Put each of the unanswered on your personal "to do" list and add anything else that is necessary for you to complete it. If the task is too big on its own, begin by cutting the large task up into smaller tasks and list little things you can do each day to further progress.

Paul teaches us much about true freedom and its call to action. Read 1 cor 9:19. Does Paul believe that he has freedom? _____ Because he is truly free, what did he decide to do with that freedom?_____
Paul goes on to clarify how he will use this slavery mentality to save souls for Christ. Look at verses 20-22. How does he serve the Jew? _____ How does he serve the weak? _____

In 1 Cor. 9:26-27, Paul shows us how he will accomplish his call from God. He knew he could not sit idle even though he was promised salvation. He compared himself to an athlete running a race. *"No, I _____ my body and _____it for fear that, after having preached to others, I myself shall be _____."*

Try this visual with me: Life is a battlefield (no problem visualizing that part, I'm sure) and Jesus owns the only fleet of choppers that can take us back home. True freedom is the comfort of knowing that Jesus has already paid for and instructed our helicopters to fly to heaven upon our death. There is no guessing or worrying, the helicopter is here and will at some point in time fly us home. All we have to do is get in and accept the free ride. What we do while we are waiting to go home is very important. He calls each of us to take part in His earthly work by continuing to fight the enemy that preys on and destroys human life. Jesus, also at work in heaven, mimics our actions and matches our pace on earth to his pace in heaven, as he prepares each of our eternal dwelling places. Read this passage to understand Paul's perspective on our heavenly compensation plan:

The one who plants and the one who waters are equal, and each will receive wages in proportion to his labor. For we are God's co-workers; you are God's field, God's building. According to the grace of God given to me, like a wise master builder I laid a foundation, and another is building upon it. But each one must be careful how he builds upon it, for no one can lay a foundation other than the one that is there, namely, Jesus Christ. If anyone builds on this foundation with gold, silver, precious stones, wood, hay, or straw, the work of each will come to light, for the Day will disclose it. It will be revealed with fire, and the fire (itself) will test the quality of each one's work. If the work stands that someone built upon the foundation, that person will receive a wage. But if someone's work is burned up, that one will suffer loss; the person will be saved, but only as through fire. Do you not know that you are the temple of God, and that the Spirit of God dwells in you? If anyone destroys God's temple, God will destroy that person; for the temple of God, which you are, is holy. (1 Corinthians 3:8 -17)

Getting back to the helicopter analogy, Paul accepted the free ride to heaven, but as he was about to settle in to his seat, strap himself in and order a drink, he turned in humility toward the battlefield he left behind. He stared in amazement that so many others had not also run to the helicopter and the free ride that awaited them. He observed that many lay wounded fighting for their lives while others just wondered aimlessly through the dangerous terrain. Paul instantly jumped out and ran back and forth from the battlefield to the helicopter, picked up, led, helped or carried as many souls as possible to their seats and to safety. It was not long before he noticed some of the people he had helped would now leave to help others and some used their skills to stay inside and administer to the wounded. Did Paul <u>risk</u> or <u>make</u> his life by reentering the perilous battlefield? _____

What kind of celebration do you think was going on in the helicopter as it took off for heaven?

_____

Any thoughts on the reception this full and joyful helicopter received upon arrival in Heaven and what Paul's final dwelling may look like? _____

_____

_____

_____

_____

_____

SUMMARY OF THE THIRD SORROW

Allow this sorrow of loss, anxiousness, and desperation to settle in. Pray that we find the comfort that our hearts lack. Pray that we are enlightened about and find understanding in the extreme, yet essential, sacrifice of the Passover lamb. May we seek and honor the will of God as we wander this temporary dwelling place on Earth awaiting our reunion with our Creator at His glorious feast.

Please take a moment to record what you learned about our Heavenly Queen and Mother during this sorrow. You may want to include a thought about her model faith in God.

_____

_____

_____

_____

_____

Let us pray:

Hail Mary, full of Grace. The Lord is with you.

Blessed are you among women, and blessed is the fruit of your womb, Jesus.

Holy Mary, Mother of God, pray for us sinners, now and at the hour of our death. Amen.

The Meeting of Jesus and Mary
on the Way of the Cross

the fourth sorrow

Read Luke 23: 26-32

I cannot imagine how it must have felt to follow Jesus, to watch him first be flogged, stripped, mimicked, and crowned with piercing thorns. Then to watch him embrace, carry and struggle beneath the heaviness of the wooden cross, laden with the sins of the world. Luke clearly teaches us here and throughout his gospel that as disciples of Christ we, like Simon the Cyrenian, must embrace, bear, and help carry the cross at times. Like the large crowd who followed him, when we do not have a cross to bear, we are to walk beside and support the ones who do. By helping Jesus carry the cross we cannot help but to follow in our Savior's footsteps. By standing in support of him, we cannot help but deepen our own understanding while providing strength and encouragement to the one who suffers. *1 Peter 2: 21 For to this you have been called, because Christ also suffered for you, leaving you an example that you should follow in his footsteps.*

MARY'S ROLE

Where is Mary in all of this? Mary understood her role throughout this walk of agony and tears and teaches us much about the bond we must have with our Lord and each other. Her role was not to bury herself in sorrows at home, nor to seek and allow loved ones to comfort her, nor to find solace in the temple and pray for strength for her son. It was her role to be at his side and the reason for it and the lesson it provides are enormous.

Because of her compassion, Mary's thoughts would have been for Jesus alone, his excruciating pain with each step, and the horrible death that awaited him at Calvary. She would have turned her thoughts to his fears and his anguish and she would have sought to console or share his pain. She would have prayed fervently for him as she too walked the long and narrow streets knowing that her son needed something only she could give.

To onlookers, she may have been only one woman among a large crowd, but her specific purpose to make herself visible to her suffering son would have been critical. For her loving eyes would be whom Jesus' tired eyes would seek; his wont gaze would finally find a familiar comfort. From this devoted, faithful, and true woman, Jesus' weakened and beaten body would gain strength. For within a moment of Mary's gaze Jesus would have found answers he so desperately sought since his visit to the garden the previous evening. An entire conversation can be exchanged with one glance into a compassionate soul and Jesus would have discovered the fountain of newfound energy needed to replenish his weary and spent body. Unfortunately, almost as fast as he could fill the void, the extended fatigue and insurmountable torment would have absorbed his satisfying treasure. He would find himself bringing back to mind his mother's sweetness and the eyes and actions into which he found a moment of refuge and the clear window into His proud and loving Father.

God calls us to be that refuge at times. He shows Himself through us and he asks that we not diminish this necessary and important work. As children we understood this need and sought our parents faces from every stage, field, or court we embarked upon. It was their face that we needed to see when the nightmare woke us up or our fever rose or our stomach ached. We found comfort in knowing that they were there for us. As we grew in independence we also began to doubt both our need for refuge and our ability to provide it. As adults we can easily forget how powerful and crucial this refuge can be in bonding to acquaintances, friends, and even our own children. Sometimes we try to justify our absence because we talk ourselves into believing that our presence isn't important. Sometimes we pity ourselves into thinking that we will not be missed. Sometimes we convince ourselves that we are too busy.

Mary's presence was critical to Jesus' Way of the Cross. Trust God, not yourself, when he tugs at you to be present for him. You are needed.

Whose face gives you refuge? Describe the feeling? _____

_____

_____

Who do you know (hope) that you provide refuge for? _____

_____

How do you do it, in other words, what is your trademark on compassion? We may do it without thinking about it, (i.e., a compassionate smile, good listener, share a meal, an unexpected call, send a card) but nevertheless we do have a particular way in which we like to invite others into our hearts to find refuge. Think about it and then document some of your favorites:

_____

_____

EMBRACING THE CROSS

In the movie Passion of the Christ, it was pointed out to me during a study that the actor portraying Jesus embraced or hugged the cross when it was first handed over to him. The class sat in amazement as we watched the scene played out again. The beaten, scourged, stripped, and humiliated man who still wore a crown of thorns atop his bloodstained head grabbed for the cross as if it were a long lost friend. What I had missed before was now so clear to me and the image, ingrained in my mind and written on my heart, comes to mind often when I have a task to do and feel like pouting my way through it. This is the mental dialog that has so often crept into my mind and takes me as far away from Mary's role and Jesus' embrace as I could possibly get.

> Me: "Why not embrace this begrudged task? Cause I am exhausted at the mere thought. I can think of a million other things I'd rather be doing and I doubt that my effort will make any difference. The complainers are the ones who get the sympathy- at least to a point. Why embrace it? Someone might overlook that there is some true s-u-f-f-e-r-i-n-g going on here! What if my humility is misread for enjoyment? Furthermore, what if they are ungrateful or overlook, dismiss, or criticize my hard labor and efforts? How can they be so ungrateful?"

Don't we sometimes do the same to Christ? Was everyone grateful over 2000 years ago who watched as Jesus accepted his unjust Crucifixion so that we, and even the very ones crucifying him, should be forgiven? No. Is everyone grateful now? No. How wonderful and noteworthy it must be for him when we do stop to remember to be grateful, to say thank you, and to just sit in his presence, reassuring him that his sacrifice was not in vain.

Do we take the time to simply and purposefully sit with Jesus? That brings me to another holy and healing Catholic tradition. Eucharistic Adoration. Like the rosary, daily Mass, meditating on the Sorrows, or thoughtful prayer, Adoration gives us another way to abide in him and feel his closeness every day. Catholic tradition offers us so many avenues to our Divine God. Some churches have perpetual Adoration, some weekly or monthly, and some are not able to offer it at all, but if you can go, GO! For many years I did not know what Adoration was, so I will define it for you. Eucharistic Adoration is when the Consecrated Host, or Body of Jesus, is displayed in a monstrance for worship. It is a powerful way to be blessed and to just visit, sit, pray with, or talk to Jesus.

Catholic Link

Catechism of the Catholic Church

2628

Adoration is the first attitude of man acknowledging that he is a creature before his Creator. It exalts the greatness of the Lord who made us and the almighty power of the Savior who sets us free from evil. Adoration is homage of the spirit to the "King of Glory," respectful silence in the presence of the "ever greater" God. Adoration of the thrice-holy and sovereign God of love blends with humility and gives assurance to our supplications.

If you have experienced Eucharistic Adoration, would you mind writing some adjectives here that describe your time in front of the Blessed Sacrament? _____

_____

_____

Is there a cross you dread bearing? _____ If so, why do you dread it?

_____

_____

_____

Is there someone you know, other than Jesus, who has demonstrated to you that the cross can be embraced rather than scorned? (Many times I try to think of our country's brave heroes, the saints who blazed trails for us, and those who battle a terminal illness with grace and determination, but it can be as simple as the person next door who never complains, even when they should or could, and is always welcoming to you and your family.) Write your thoughts here:

_____

_____

_____

In studying Christ's suffering we can begin visualizing the passion with which our Savior must have taken up, no, embraced, the cross for our salvation.

KEEPING THE WOOD GREEN

Let's read verse 31 again (Luke 23:31). How do we keep the wood of the cross from drying out, vulnerable to a single flame, burned into ashes, and swept away with the winds of evil? How do we keep it fresh in our hearts and minds, "ever-green", if you will? Mary knows and is teaching us the very way in which to breathe it in every day, meditate on it, study it, let it live in us, and share it with others. John explains this by using Jesus' own analogy of the Vine and the Branches. Let's turn to John 15:1-9 to reacquaint ourselves with the message. Jesus tells us exactly how to keep the wood green, so to speak. Let's play "fill in the blank" and "multiple choice" to make sure it sets in.

First, who is God? (v.1) _____ Jesus is the(v.1)_____.
Jesus asks us simply to (v4) _____ in him as he _____ in us.

Why must we remain in him, the vine? (v.4-6) (check all that apply) 0 To bear fruit, 0 To remain on the vine, 0 To not wither and be cast out, 0 To eat ice cream *(Did I catch you?)*

What two things must happen for the bond to be complete? (v 7) *"If you _____ ____ _____ and _____ _____ remain in you..."* Huh? This states that the bond is broken only one way. It does not say that *you* must remain in *me* and *me* in *you* because Jesus' end *will never be broken*. It says that we must remain in him and that his words must remain in us. Both are things that we are in control of. So let me get this straight, to have a bond with Jesus we must:

remain in his powerful, secure and strong arms and
let his loving words nestle into our hearts and minds.

We then will be able to: *"ask for _____ we _____*

and it will be _____ for us." (v 7)

Sign me up! That sounds great.

So why is it so hard?

To allow or invite all these to happen we must exhibit disciplined behaviors and make some conscious efforts to stay with God. Because of free will we must choose it or accept it continuously so it can take up residence within our hearts. Although we know it is true and we have even experienced it at times (when his strong and mighty arms held onto us through a tough night or season) we still mess up. We still give in at times. We still walk away and try to make it without God and then, dear friends, is when we have the audacity to ask Jesus to keep his promise and give us whatever we want only to be dispirited when he seems to ignore our demand. That is not how Jesus works. It is difficult to accept but we know that it is a familiar pattern of human behavior. When we are truly secured in his loving arms and his words are bonded to our actions and thoughts, do you know what happens? Our wants change. Imagine that! What we want is also what he wants for us because we are one with him. That is when true happiness exists and our requests are done for us.

Catholic Link

The Catholic Mass

Doxology and Great Amen:

Priest: Through him, with him, and in him, in the unity of the Holy Spirit, all glory and honor is yours, almighty Father, for ever and ever.

All: Amen!

THROUGH HIM, WITH HIM, IN HIM

One with him. During our Mass, at the conclusion of the Consecration, the priest utters the familiar Doxology in which we respond with the Great Amen. I am ashamed to say that when I was younger these words meant only that relief from kneeling and staying still was moments away. Hooray! Now my hooray has a different motive. It is because I understand the miracle that has just taken place on the altar before me and that even though I am not worthy to receive him, I may be made worthy by his healing approval of me. I am minutes away from the personal "Amen" which will allow his Body and his Blood to touch me, heal me, and live in me. To me, this moment serves as an Earthly prelude to the great wonders that will be introduced and revealed to us in Heaven.

The words of our beautiful and heavenly Catholic Mass can be found scattered throughout the Bible. The more time spent reading, the better I understand the wisdom, intricacies, and depth of the Sacred Liturgy. The symbolism of the incense, candles, tabernacle, and even robes of the priest are scribed upon the pages of the Book that gives us life. In other words, for years I was content with scrutinizing only the tip of the iceberg, never realizing its immense span of support beneath the water. We owe it to ourselves and to future generations to search the depths and do our homework, for it is there that we become convicted in the foundation of the Catholic faith. Let's check two places for the words of the Doxology that we have just been studying, and dive into them before we close this sorrow.

What similarities do you see between the above Doxology and Romans 11:36? _____

_____

_____

The following passage from Colossians is longer and poetic in its description of our deliverance **through him**. Let Paul's message sink in and know that our Mass, our walk **with him,** or taking up the cross behind him, will all keep our faith strong **in him.** Consume Colossians 1: 13-23, then fill the blanks to cement the message upon your minds and to fill your hearts with God's great love for us.

(verse 13) "*He delivered us from the* _____

_____ *and transferred us to* _____

_____ "

(verse 16) *For* **in him** *were created* _____ *in heaven and on earth, the visible and the invisible, whether thrones or dominions or principalities or powers;* _____ *were created* **through him** *and* **for him**.

(verse 17) *He is before all things, and in him* _____

_____. Have you ever felt like a piece of you was broken inside, perhaps torn out, or that the world was crumbling around you? Somehow, our once happy spirit comes to a screeching halt, quickly plummets, or shatters into pieces. Isn't it a great reminder that, "*In Him all things hold together.*"

Paul tells us in verse 21 that we: "*...once were alienated and hostile in mind because of our evil deeds...*" Verse 22 describes how we have been reconciled by Jesus' death. This reconciliation allows us to be presented as worthy. How will we be presented? (verse 22) 0 as holy 0 without blemish 0 irreproachable

Isn't it awesome that our sins can be wiped clean because of Jesus? God loves us "as is" on Earth but only the holy, unblemished, and irreproachable can enter into the kingdom of God. Jesus paid the price for our salvation. Sounds easy, huh? Is there a catch? What does verse 23 say about how we must act to be assured the prize? Summarize your thoughts here:

_____

_____

_____

SUMMARY OF THE FOURTH SORROW

My mother told me once that she never understood why God had chosen to take Joseph to heaven knowing that Mary would have to face this day without his support, love and help. Magnified at Lent, as she would pray the Stations of the Cross, she would ask God to help her understand why he would do that to Mary. While deeply praying one time this thought came to her and she passed it on to me.

Joseph was an honorable and righteous man who was granted many gifts and skills to be the husband of the Mother of God and the earthly father to the Son of God. This was no easy job, but Joseph performed as protector, provider, and mentor flawlessly. Joseph knew well his role as protector of Mary and Jesus and would have stopped at nothing to keep them safe. Joseph also understood his role as provider and had used his carpentry skills to provide for their young family's needs throughout Israel and Egypt. He also understood his role as mentor and would have passed both his skills and his integrity on to Jesus throughout his boyhood.

Everything that God had instilled in Joseph to do went against what would now need to be done. Joseph could not have stood by and watched as Jesus was wrongly accused. Joseph could not have allowed them to scourge, beat, mock and crown his son with thorns. Joseph would not have been able to watch his son carry the cross to his death. He was not wired that way. He was his protector, provider, and mentor, and therefore, his job had been completed. No longer was Jesus to be protected. No longer would he require any provisions except from his Father in Heaven, and God would be the only one who could mentor Jesus through the Agony in the Garden and the footsteps to the cross.

God was there all the time, but he has "this thing" about using other people to help us see Him, know Him, choose Him, and love Him. If someone is carrying a cross beside you and needs to see God's hope, then show them hope. If you struggle beneath a cross, allow someone to help you with the burden. Ask God to help us embrace our cross and to remember that the ultimate cross of our salvation has already been carried for us.

What did you learn about Mary in this chapter? You may want to include thoughts on "being present" and allowing others to see God through her. What about her faith in this sorrow?

_____

_____

_____

_____

Did you learn anything about yourself in this chapter? If so, record some thoughts here.

_____

_____

_____

Let us pray:

Hail Mary, full of Grace. The Lord is with you.

Blessed are you among women, and blessed is the fruit of your womb, Jesus.

Holy Mary, Mother of God, pray for us sinners, now and at the hour of our death. Amen.

The Crucifixion

the fifth sorrow

Read with new eyes John 19: 16-30.

I cannot even say this sorrow without feeling the need to bow my head or sink to my knees. No matter how many times I pray it, I hope to never lose the tremendous humility and reverence this sorrow stirs in me. Jesus' crucifixion was the immeasurable price he willingly paid for you and me to have salvation. Our sins, which were nailed to that cross along with our Savior, are as unique to us as his perfectly tailored love is that covers those imperfections. My words, therefore, would fall short in expressing what you solely know to be true and what has been written upon your heart. Put yourself at the foot of the cross and please take some time to acknowledge his immense love for you. Scribe your own thought or prayer here before we begin.

_____

_____

_____

_____

_____

The crucifixion was foretold in the Old Testament, revealed and fulfilled in the New Testament, and is integral to our Catholic faith and tradition. We will study some of the symbolism, signs, and representations that link this day to historical writings, New Testament Covenant, and our present day liturgy. You might say that this sorrow, in essence, sets the very table at which we, who were not worthy before Christ, are now made worthy to be "called to his supper."

Catholic Link

The Catholic Mass

Communion:

Priest: Behold the Lamb of God, behold him who takes away the sins of the world. Blessed are those called to the supper of the Lamb.

All: Lord, I am not worthy that you should enter under my roof, but only say the word and my soul shall be healed.

With all the instruction that lays ahead of us, let's look to our mother, Mary, for guidance and clarification. Allowing Mary to take us back to the foot of the cross, she will teach us what we need to understand and lead our hearts to pray along with her.

MARY AT THE FOOT OF THE CROSS

Mary was there, at the foot of the cross, looking up in anticipation and helplessness at his bleeding, suffering, and thirsting body. Wondering, now, if what she just witnessed could somehow be a nightmare. Flashbacks would ensue of the arrest of her innocent son. Then to his submission to being scourged and beaten beyond recognition, crowned with thorns, mocked, tormented, stripped and spit upon. She watched as he embraced the cross for us, fell under its weight, and was led to the slaughter like a lamb. Then she felt and heard the deafening sound as the nails sliced through his hands and his feet. She would cringe as His body was hoisted in the air and jolted into place, as she knew the pain would be unrelenting now. Every breath would now be laborious and more difficult with time. Even his garments would cause discussion among the four soldiers and eventually they would choose to cast lots for his seamless tunic. Mary would watch, listen, and pray as her Son was made a spectacle of, wondering when God would take their Son home. He would suffer for hours before she would finally watch him die and, through all of this, she would never leave his side.

No matter how much she knew about this day and no matter how Jesus may have carefully and lovingly prepared his mother for his brutal assignment, it must have been an overwhelming site to behold. Can you imagine a worse sting to your heart? The fifth arrow would have found no rest, but would have sought to relentlessly wound her, as never before, in a place she had not known to exist until this moment. This sharp and penetrating arrow no doubt drilled deeper and was more pervasive than any other. How could it be any other way? What pain for a mother could ever measure to this? Fresh tears would have filled her eyes, as reality of everything that was happening to her innocent Son would come to the surface. Yes, she would have been strong and would have placed her unquestioning faith in God's ultimate plan, yet she would weep for her beloved Son and the Savior of the World.

Do you think it possible, that it may have been at Jesus' *hour of death*, that Mary would come to understand her unique gift from God? Then she would ask His permission to commit herself to her Sons followers that we also may never know death without her comfort and fervent prayers. What a loving Mother we have in Mary, who would extend similar consolations to us, the lowly sinners.

Holy Mary, Mother of God, pray for us sinners, now and at the hour of our death.

and her 6th grace for us states:

I will visibly help them at the moment of their death; they will see the face of their mother.

Yes, I want this woman, who honed her skills of compassion and comfort on our Savior, to be at my side! I long to see the pleasing comfort in her face and to hear the prayers she declares for me and utters with me as I transition from this death to everlasting life. I pray this also for you, and know that we can trust that Mary will follow through. Just as she did for Jesus, she too will do for us.

Think of some ways that you have been honored by someone's presence in a time of need. Did you realize their importance immediately or did the significance hit you later? Explain.

_____

_____

_____

_____

Simply by their nature, some professions or jobs will confront more people at their hour of death than the normal human being will ever witness. Medical fields, caretakers of the elderly, police, firefighters, priests, and our enlisted men and women all have been called to a mission that may require the extraordinary. They may be given the chance to hear-out and give comfort to God's child as they pass over to eternal life.

Have you ever been with someone when they died? If you can recall a thought or wisdom taken from that experience, please write it here. _____

_____

_____

_____

BIBLICAL REFERENCE TO THE CRUCIFIXION

The Scripture that you read at the beginning of this sorrow holds some key information for us. Let's dissect it to learn more about why recording the events of this day into the Gospels would help frame our holy church, place Mary as our beloved Mother, and convince present and future generations that Jesus was indeed the Messiah promised in the Old Testament. Turn to John 19: 16-30

John 19:23-24 compares to Psalms 22:19 in what way? _____

_____

John 19: 26 is our benchmark for the next passage and instruction for our church. Many scholars along with the Catholic Church agree that these last words of instruction from Jesus were extremely significant just as the last words are for many dying human beings. With Jesus' proclamation of Mary as "Woman" he takes us immediately back to two stories, one in the Book of Genesis and one in the Gospel of John. Let's first look all the way back to Genesis 2:23 which states:

the man said: "This one, at last, is bone of my bones and flesh of my flesh;
This one shall be called 'woman,' for out of 'her man' this one has been taken."

Mary is the New Covenant "Woman" in that she immaculately conceived and gave birth to God's son and bone of their bone and flesh of their flesh, but this One shall be called the "Son of Man," for out of "her" this One has been taken.

I remember the first time I heard someone speak on the subject of Mary as the new "Eve," and it seems that since then, so many questions have been answered for me. I have been able to understand with more clarity the next passage that used to boggle my mind. It is a very familiar story to all of us but one line holds new meaning for me now. I'll explain. The setting is the wedding in Cana and Jesus had not yet performed his first miracle. Mary informs Jesus that they have no wine. So here is the line: John 2:4

(And) Jesus said to her, "Woman, how does your concern affect me? My hour has not yet come."

First, I thought Jesus was being a little disrespectful here calling his Mom, Woman; and furthermore, I wondered if Mary was being a little pushy. My answer follows:

Now flashback to Genesis again, 3:12-13.

The man replied, "The woman whom you put here with me--
she gave me fruit from the tree, so I ate it."
The LORD God then asked the woman, "Why did you do such a thing?"
The woman answered, "The serpent tricked me into it, so I ate it."

The link below beautifully illustrates how God not only did not abandon us after the fall of man, but he sent Jesus and Mary to overcome the evils of original sin. In the Old Testament, the triangle of evil was Adam, Eve, and the serpent. In the New Testament, the triangle of good is Jesus, Mary, and God. Through this we are restored to His grace.

Catholic Link

Catechism of the Catholic Church

"You Did Not Abandon Him to the Power of Death"

410
After his fall, man was not abandoned by God. On the contrary, God calls him and in a mysterious way heralds the coming victory over evil and his restoration from his fall. This passage in Genesis is called the Protoevangelium ("first gospel"): the first announcement of the Messiah and Redeemer, of a battle between the serpent and the Woman, and of the final victory of a descendant of hers.

411
The Christian tradition sees in this passage an announcement of the "New Adam" who, because he "became obedient unto death, even death on a cross," makes amends superabundantly for the disobedience of Adam. Furthermore many Fathers and Doctors of the Church have seen the woman announced in the Protoevangelium as Mary, the mother of Christ, the "new Eve." Mary benefited first of all and uniquely from Christ's victory over sin: she was preserved from all stain of original sin and by a special grace of God committed no sin of any kind during her whole earthly life.

Eve urged Adam to participate in the act against God. The new woman, Mary, also requested something of her man, Jesus, and the man again acquiesced. This time, however, the serpent did not win. The team of Jesus and Mary would continually outwit the lowly serpent. This new man and this new woman, through a single exchange that became the prelude of what was to come, conquered the original sin of Adam and Eve. Mankind faired much better in this story than in the one of Genesis. Jesus became our Savior and Mary became the loving Mother of our Church.

Let's finish the story we started and be delighted that Jesus, who **is** the "good wine," was saved for last. This was revealed so that all may know his Salvation.

John 2:5-11 *His mother said to the servers, "Do whatever he tells you." Now there were six stone water jars there for Jewish ceremonial washings, each holding twenty to thirty gallons. Jesus told them, "Fill the jars with water." So they filled them to the brim. Then he told them, "Draw some out now and take it to the headwaiter." So they took it.*

And when the headwaiter tasted the water that had become wine, without knowing where it came from (although the servers who had drawn the water knew), the headwaiter called the bridegroom and said to him, "Everyone serves good wine first, and then when people have drunk freely, an inferior one; but you have kept the good wine until now." Jesus did this as the beginning of his signs in Cana in Galilee and so revealed his glory, and his disciples began to believe in him.

John 19:28 has what in common with Psalm 22:16? _____
_____

John 19:29 is interesting and shares more than just a word with **Exodus 12:22**. First let's find the word and then we'll study the significance. Looking at both passages below, find the name of the plant that was used for dipping into the blood and was again used to raise a wine soaked sponge to our Lord's mouth. Record the plant name here _____

Exodus 12:22 Then take a bunch of hyssop, and dipping it in the blood that is in the basin, sprinkle the lintel and the two doorposts with this blood. But none of you shall go outdoors until morning.

John 19:29 There was a vessel filled with common wine. So they put a sponge soaked in wine on a sprig of hyssop and put it up to his mouth.

The hyssop plant serves as one link from the old to new covenants. Remember from the third Sorrow, the hyssop (a willowy type of plant) was used in Exodus to cover the doorway with blood of the lamb so that the Jewish believers may be "passed over" by the plague of death.

At the crucifixion, the sponge was soaked in wine and the hyssop again was used. This time, to elevate it to the perfect Lamb of God's mouth (signifying that Jesus' blood will cover the new covenant doorposts and will serve as our security that eternal death will "pass over" his believers. We then will be free to enjoy eternal life with God. We also learned in the third sorrow, through the Catholic Link, that Christian Funerals are also called "The Christian's Last Passover" because Jesus reenacted, reclaimed, and then fulfilled the Passover feast with His death upon the cross.

LINKING OTHER SCRIPTURE PASSAGES

There are many references of the life, Passion, and resurrection of Christ scattered throughout the Old Testament. Each of the 4 Gospels contains the Crucifixion. We began with John's account of this period because it includes some additional detail and has reference to the Old Testament. Besides looking further into John, we will visit a few other gospels to see what we can find. Draw a line to link the foretelling verse to the proper gospel passage.

OLD TESTAMENT	NEW TESTAMENT
Psalms 22:2	Matthew 27:34
Exodus 12:46	Mark 15:34
Isaiah 50:6	John 19:33
Zechariah 12:10	John 19:34
Psalms 69:22	Matthew 27: 30-31

Jesus didn't leave it up to the apostles to figure all of this out on their own. In Luke 24:44 we read:

> He said to them, "These are my words that I spoke to you while I was still with you, that everything written about me in the law of Moses and in the prophets and psalms must be fulfilled."

I am amazed at the intricacies and complexities woven into the Bible and how each generation of people can read new meaning and clarity into what was written thousands of years ago. Will we ever possess all the answers to this mysterious collection of historical books? I think not --- for the Bible is to me like the great depths of the ocean yet to be explored. Scientists speculate and debate the deepness of the ocean's trenches and continue to be surprised at the confirmation of life existing nearly 7 miles below the earth's surface. (Farther under sea level than Mt. Everest's peak is above.) Modern technology may allow myths or theories to be replaced with fact, yet the answers many times yield only more questions. The darkness and distance make every clue, albeit rewarding, a time consuming proposition. We cannot see the bottom of these deep and narrow depressions and no man has ever touched its floor yet we have faith that it exists.

The ocean depths are similar to the mysteries of the Bible in that we know enough of its surface and contents to be dangerous! We possess maps, which identify their vast surfaces just as we have the Bible as our map of God's Word. It is not until we sail through their living waters, plunge their depths, float in their calmness, and fear their relentless destruction that we can truly come to know them. The nourishment they provide is satisfying and we have found solace in their tempo yet we yearn for more understanding. Many lives over much time have been both dedicated and surrendered to their mysteries, yet we still lack resolution. The mysteries remain locked inside their depths.

Is it frustrating? No, it simply magnifies His eminence and that our awe and reverence are well placed at His feet.

SUMMARY OF THE FIFTH SORROW

As we let this most sorrowful of sorrows settle into our hearts let us thank Mary for being visible unto her own Son's, and our Savior's, death. We ask to know her sweetness always and may we never forget the power we hold over our enemies when we abide in her Son through his gift of the Holy Spirit. As a pouch of tea transforms a kettle of water may, too, our minds, hearts, and bodies be transformed by steeping in God's Word. Never let us forget the price that was paid for our souls and that it includes an invitation to a heavenly inheritance.

Oh God our Father, help us in our journey to accept the call to His supper and remind us often of the gifts we were given to share with others. Allow us to be a beacon of light to the lowly, sick, and needy; we implore you to work through us and use us to deliver your most precious comforts to our world.

What was Mary's lesson to you as you studied her fifth sorrow? You may want to include what Mary taught you as you placed yourself at the foot of the cross and the significance of Mary as the Mother of the Catholic Church.

_____

_____

_____

_____

How does Mary differ from Eve?

_____

_____

_____

Let us pray:

Hail Mary, full of Grace. The Lord is with you.

Blessed are you among women, and blessed is the fruit of your womb, Jesus.

Holy Mary, Mother of God, pray for us sinners, now and at the hour of our death. Amen.

The Taking Down of the Body of Jesus from the Cross

the sixth sorrow

Read Mark 15:42-47.

It's curious to me how none of the gospels belabor Jesus being taken down from the cross; however, so many artists have been inspired to paint or carve this time into history. Possibly it is because no words could describe these moments, yet a picture can tell a thousand words.

All the gospels include at least a few sentences about it, and they each credit Joseph of Arimathea for asking Pilate for the body of Jesus. As we do our research for this sorrow we will spend some time understanding Joseph and what he must have meant to our Holy Lady on this day.

We will also take a closer look at Jesus' life, through Mary's eyes. As I have meditated on this sorrow a single common thread has uncompromisingly woven itself into my mind. That is, that as Mary held her lifeless son, she would have undoubtedly pressed into memory the other occasions in which she held him---- at his birth, fleeing to Egypt, as he slept as a child, when he needed comfort, and then now. When was the last time she had held him like this? Was it when she rocked him to sleep as a baby or did he come to her lap often as a child? Whenever it was, it was probably not noted as such. How many kids say, "Hey mom, this is the last time I am going to crawl up into your lap, so enjoy it?" It just happens slowly over time and most of the memories fade, and then meld together in a kind of abstract portrayal of time gone by. It would only be the "special occasion" memories that would bring her clarity at this moment and she would cherish each image as it flashed before her. Induced by sadness, these precious memories would serve her like a healing salve upon her pierced and wounded heart.

A CLOSER LOOK AT JOSEPH

As stated above, Joseph was somewhat of a "Savior" sent to Mary and Jesus that day. I wonder who might have sent him? Any ideas? _____. I think so too, that God first prevented or obstructed his presence in Jerusalem and then timed his arrival back into town. Let's see what clues the Gospels hold for us.

Starting with the one you read above, what does Mark 15:43 tell us about Joseph?

Joseph was from: 0 Nazareth   0 Bethlehem   0 Arimathea

and a _____ _____ of the council.

He was awaiting the _____ ____ _____.

He approached Pilate in what way? 0 Timid   0 Courageous   0 Threatening

What did he ask for? _____

(Verse 45) After confirming that Jesus was already dead, Pilate: 0 denied him his body

0 gave him the body   0 turned the body over to the Jewish leaders

(Verse 46) Joseph bought a: 0 burial plot   0 linen cloth   0 flowers

Joseph took him _____. (This action alone makes me sigh--- we will talk more about it later)

He wrapped him and he laid him in the tomb. (We will talk in more detail about these actions in the next sorrow.)

Now to Matthew's account. Review Matthew 27:57 to fill in more about this Godly man. He came back into town at what time of day? _____

He was: 0 poor   0 middle class   0 rich

He was a _____ of Jesus.

Seek Luke's words and insight in chapter 23, verses 50 and 51.

He called Joseph: 0 virtuous and righteous   0 wealthy   0 cowardly

Luke mentions that Joseph was a member of the council but that he had not _____
_____. Interesting, huh!

John gives us even a little more depth to this man. Let's find it in John 19:38. What secret did Joseph keep? _____ Why did he need to keep it a secret?

_____

_____

This is quite a bit of information for a man who was no more than a blip on the radar screen. I contend that his role was esteemed and regarded. Here he was, a member of the council that had just hours ago condemned Jesus to death, and he returns to town to hear of the astonishing news. Despite his secret discipleship and fear of conflict, he courageously faces Pilate to ask for Jesus' body. Would it not have been easier for him to walk away and deny his following? What compelled him to do these wondrous things for Mary, the other women, and men who stood helplessly waiting as Jesus' body hung lifeless upon the cross? No one else would have possessed the authority to go straight to Pilate for an answer with such resolve. The entire chain of events has God's fingerprints all over it and I can't help but imagine that it was in answer to his beloved Mary's prayer.

Can you remember a recent time when things miraculously fell into place? Sometimes God is subtle in his gifts and other times he leaves us a blinking neon sign reminding us of his helping hand. Describe as many miracles as you care to, for in remembering them we feel His warmth and love.

_____

_____

_____

_____

MARY'S CLASSROOM AT THE FOOT OF THE CROSS

Let's place ourselves back at the foot of the cross. Jesus had breathed his last and a soldier, according to the gospel of John, had thrust a lance into Jesus' side. Blood and water flowed from the wound and he was pronounced dead by the soldiers. Otherwise, they would have broken his legs like they had the two criminals on either side of Jesus. The Roman soldiers would have maintained control to this point, as the sentence for crucifixion would not end until its completion was certified.

Mary knew it was over but would wait helplessly for approval to remove his body. Even if she had been given approval, can you imagine the mental and physical difficulty of this task? Strength would be required to dislodge the nails and then to hold his body in place until it was free of all that bound him to the cross. Where would she take her son's body? I have to believe that so many answers came with the sight of Joseph. Isn't it odd that his name was the same as Mary's faithful but deceased husband? Coincidence? I don't think so! A sign? More likely!

Joseph had obtained approval for his body to be released, bought a clean linen cloth for his burial clothing, and had secured a cave nearby for his tomb.

Although we do not know through scripture what happened at this time, I will share my meditation thoughts with you and give you space to write your own.

I imagine that Mary received into her arms her beloved Son, Jesus. She wept at the sight of his fresh wounds that had been hidden from her sight. There would be too many to count yet she would take-in every bruise, cut, and tear that his body had been subjected to. His crown of thorns would be removed, but not easily, and it would expose more punctures upon his sweet head. His flesh, and then her clothes would be saturated in the blood that became our ransom. She would instinctively want to comfort and address the wounds, only to remember that his body no longer ached and was no longer submissive to the slaughter he had endured for our Salvation.

We already touched on, at the beginning of this sorrow, the memories that would have given her comfort. Although Scripture reports his modest and holy birth, that Mary carried him to the Temple for Presentation, and that her arms protected him as they fled to Egypt, we know that these narratives disclose only snippets of their intimacy. This loving Mother would have reflected on Simeon's words as she watched Jesus sleep, wondering how long she would be allowed to comfort him and asking God to bless her with as many days as He deemed possible. She would have submitted herself to his pleasure and contentment in everything that she did. She would have fulfilled her work happily and prayed earnestly. She would commit herself to keep their home peaceful and warm, relaxed and loving. She would accomplish all these things in humble and ignoble surroundings and Jesus and Joseph would want for nothing because of Mary.

This is about the time that I get hit smack between the eyes. Mary teaches us through her unpretentious and loving examples that we may know true fulfillment in our own lives. Take a closer look at Mary and **describe the behaviors you would expect to find** in each of the following. Feel the lesson in your heart as she teaches you about herself. I'll do the first one to get you started.

Through Mary's hardships: *Embracing them, requesting more hardship if it pleased God or helped someone else, offering them up to God, and being thankful--even for the hardships.*

In Mary's attitude: _____

_____

_____

When Mary set her priorities: _____

_____

_____

In Mary's work _____

_____

_____

In Mary's prayers _____

_____

_____

Mary toward her family _____

_____

_____

In Mary's service to others _____

_____

_____

In Mary's joyfulness _____

_____

_____

Certain characteristics and behaviors are pleasing to God and, although we are all knit together differently, we must admit that possessing Mary's qualities takes the edge off of even the most stressful of days, not to mention how attracted we are to others who are disciplined in these behaviors. Mary teaches and enlightens us on her obedient behaviors so that we might be able to draw from them as we contemplate our own lifestyles and choices.

Now read what you wrote using your name in place of Mary's.

How did it sound? Some probably sounded just like you and others maybe not so much! Don't misunderstand; I realize that sometimes we need Jesus' temper in us when correction is required. History does not document Mary as a drill sergeant, but I can assure you she was no pushover. Remember her persistence at the Wedding of Cana when they ran out of wine? She softly yet firmly stood her ground. Understand that milk toast is not the idea here, humility and a great passion to serve God with all of your strength is. Mary perfected both.

Maybe we are confused about how to humble ourselves. Does it mean to demean oneself, to lose self-respect, or have shame? No, quite the contrary! Maybe clearing up the meaning of humility will open up the floodgate to understanding how Mary operates and how her graces can help us. The following definitions are according to Merriam-Webster's Collgiate Dictionary, 11th Edition. (see acknowledgement page)

Beth Leonard

humiliate

> Etymology: Late Latin *humiliatus,* past participle of *humiliare,* from Latin *humilis* low —
> more at **humble**
> to reduce to a lower position in one's own eyes or others' eyes : mortify

As you can see, even though this word looks like it's of the same family, to be mortified or reduced in another's eyes has nothing to do with the humility we seek.

humble

> Etymology: Middle English, from Anglo-French, from Latin *humilis* low, humble, from *humus*
> earth; akin to Greek *chthōn* earth, *chamai* on the ground Date: 13th century

1: not proud or haughty : not arrogant or assertive

2: reflecting, expressing, or offered in a spirit of deference or submission <a *humble* apology>

3 a: ranking low in a hierarchy or scale : **insignificant** , **unpretentious b:** not costly or luxurious <a *humble* contraption>

What is the Latin word for humble? _____

What does humilis mean? _____ , _____

What does humus mean? _____

And check out the Greek meanings: "earth" and "on the ground."

Definition #1 says: **not** _____ or _____ : **not** _____
or _____

Huh? The "not" this and "not" that seems a little confusing. Wouldn't it be easier if it could be defined as what it "is" rather than what it is "not"? Perhaps this is just one of many holes in the English language where the most expressive words are simply not available. I prefer the Latin definition because of the picture it gives me. Low or humble to the earth, in other words, grounded! The more we recall that we were created out of dust and to dust we shall return, the better our perspective on life. All this talk of ground made me think about something else. Have you ever prayed lying on the ground, face down (prostrate position)? Humbling, isn't it?

A priest who had spent much time praying with and saying masses for Mother Teresa and her Sisters once spoke to a group of us. Among the amazing stories, I found one that I will hold onto until the day I die. The priest spoke of Mother Teresa's devotion and reverence for the mass and Blessed Sacrament. No surprise there. The shock came at his first mass with the Sisters. Dressed in simple yet crisp blue and white dresses, they sat, stood, or kneeled throughout the mass. What they did, they did in unison, and with devout humility for God. All was going well, and then during the Consecration it happened. A sound caught the attention of the priest as he recited his prayers. He looked up only to find that their genuine humility, reverence and love for Jesus had taken them from knee to face. Each one at the same time, bowing farther to the miracle that was taking place before them. I remember this often and sometimes it catches me from mindlessly reciting the words, "Lord I am not worthy that you should enter under my roof, but only say the word and my soul shall be healed." If Mother Teresa (now St. Teresa of Calcutta) had to be face down to ask for worthiness, I can only imagine the deepness of the crevasse that should hold my own humility.

I promised you space to write your own meditation thoughts, and as promised here is the chance. We have come so far and learned so much from our beloved Teacher. Please express any thoughts here about this reflective and sorrowful mystery. _____

_____

_____

_____

_____

_____

LAMB OF GOD, YOU TAKE AWAY THE SINS OF THE WORLD, GRANT US PEACE

Mary's emotions would have tilted and twirled as they struggled to find a place to rest. Could she weep now or had her tears dissolved into cherished memories? Would she love him even more for his unwavering obedience to His Father or should she feel anger or resentment toward his tormentors as she struggled with the realization of his viciously inflicted wounds? Would she reel in the polarity of it all? Her unblemished (sinless) Son, our Savior, being lowered from the cross he did not deserve, but yet embraced; asked to not drink from, yet fully accepted; and feared to the point of sweating blood, yet walked in perfect humility toward. She held, like a child, our Lamb from God.

Catholic Link

Catholic Link

Catechism of the Catholic Church

Christ's death is the unique and definitive sacrifice

613
Christ's death is both the Paschal sacrifice that accomplishes the definitive redemption of men, through "the Lamb of God, who takes away the sin of the world," and the sacrifice of the New Covenant, which restores man to communion with God by reconciling him to God through the "blood of the covenant, which was poured out for many for the forgiveness of sins."

614
This sacrifice of Christ is unique; it completes and surpasses all other sacrifices. First, it is a gift from God the Father himself, for the Father handed his Son over to sinners in order to reconcile us with himself. At the same time it is the offering of the Son of God made man, who in freedom and love offered his life to his Father through the Holy Spirit in reparation for our disobedience.

Jesus substitutes his obedience for our disobedience

SUMMARY OF THE SIXTH SORROW

The Lord does indeed answer prayer and Joseph was sent to Mary to relieve her immense suffering and loss. Mary graciously accepted God's gift of Joseph and allowed him to take care of the tasks at hand. She allowed him great honor in asking for, removing, purchasing linen for, and wrapping the body of Jesus, and he in turn honored her with necessary time to mourn and reflect. How many times do we mistake an answer to prayer for an interference or distraction? How many times is someone sent to help and we refuse to relinquish control? Mary continues to demonstrate that true strength is found through humility and true happiness by an unremitting trust in God. From the foot of the cross, she still has time to teach. Blessed are we who shall see the face of Mary as she, too, will hold us.

What do you want to remember about this sorrow? Include some of the insight that was refreshed or new to you as you learned from Mary, our Teacher.

_____

_____

_____

_____

What behaviors does Mary have that you need? How can you imitate her life to enrich your days on Earth?

_____

_____

_____

Let us pray:

Hail Mary, full of Grace. The Lord is with you.

Blessed are you among women, and blessed is the fruit of your womb, Jesus.

Holy Mary, Mother of God, pray for us sinners, now and at the hour of our death. Amen.

The Burial of Jesus

the seventh sorrow

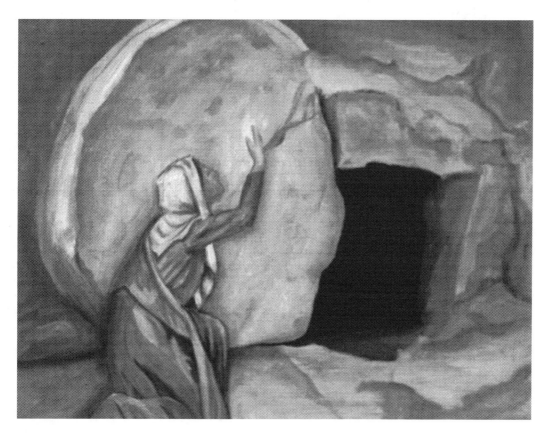

Read John 19: 39-42.

Scripture allows us only a glimpse at Jesus' burial, but our hearts know that this time would have been especially difficult for Mary. The fresh wounds from the last three sorrows still ached as her gentle heart prepared for the inevitable arrow already in flight to meet her. She again would rely on and put trust in Joseph, her gift from God, to handle some of the things she could not. She would participate in some ways and yield in other ways to those who felt the need to pay honor to their Savior. For some time now, Mary had understood Jesus' universal mantle and supported him through his work and travels. Jesus would have morphed from boy to man and thus his dependence would have melted away. On several occasions throughout the Bible, Jesus would seek refuge or some "downtime," but not at home and not with friends. He sought it alone and in prayer. Mary would have graciously understood all of this and would often leave him to his Father's call, but not on this day and not at this hour. Today, there would be no leaving his side as she stepped confidently and bravely into the direct path of the last screaming arrow directed toward her heart.

BURIALS IN SCRIPTURE

Burying the dead is recorded throughout the Bible and understanding its significance allows us to better relate to this sorrow. Therefore, we will turn some pages as we discover the importance placed on burial customs and possibly even bring new light to our present day ceremonies and traditions.

Genesis 23:1-9 teaches us about Abraham as he sought a place to bury his wife, Sarah.

According to verse 2, was Abraham familiar with the mourning rites or did he make it up as he went along? _____

_____

Verse 3 says that he had to leave her side, leading us to assume that part of the ritual was to stay by the side of the dead ones for at least a portion of time.

Why did Abraham need to address the Hittites? (v. 4)

_____

Why did the Hittites believe Abraham worthy enough to bury his wife among their own? (v. 6)

_____

_____

What kind of plot did they offer Abraham? (v. 6)

_____

Why do you think that Abraham did not simplify the matter and just take any burial ground? (v. 7-9)

_____

_____

_____

The "notes" section of my Bible shed some additional light onto these passages. Abraham, being a long-term alien but not a native to the area, still would not have had rights to purchase land among the Hittites. Because of their respect for him, they offered him land as a gift, but Abraham wished to make this his permanent home. Therefore, he chose this opportunity to legally request property among them so that his descendants would have this, albeit small, stake of property. This was the land of Canaan that God had led Abraham to. In the following verses, Abraham completes the legal purchase in front of Ephron's town council and buried Sarah in the cave of the field of Machpelah. In essence, Sarah's death brought new life to this family by allowing them to purchase a parcel of land that facilitated a family first and a new beginning. Abraham would follow Sarah in death and would be buried next to her.

Next let's seek the book of Tobit, a book retained in Catholic Bibles, for some additional wisdom and understanding. Women should especially enjoy the instructions Tobit gave to his son! Read **Tobit 4: 1-4.** Verse 3 describes the kind of burial Tobit asks for. What is it?

_____

The rest of verse 3 are wise words shared father-to-son and verse 4 holds the guilt trip! I just love it, and we thought we invented it. The last part of the verse is a sweet demand. What is it?

_____

_____

_____

Sirach, another book retained in Catholic Bibles, has a timeless step-by-step plan for burying the dead. Turn to **Sirach 38: 16-23** to fill in the following.

Step one: Shed tears *"with wailing and* _____ _____.*"*

Step two: Prepare the _____.

Step three: Do not be _____ from his burial.

Step four: *Weeping* _____, *mourning* _____, *pay your tribute of* _____, *as he deserves.* How long should this last to prevent gossip? _____

_____

Step five: After the grief, what are you to do?_____ What can happen if grief is prolonged? _____

_____

Step six: Instead of thinking of him, we should turn our thoughts to the end. What holds no hope for us left here without him? _____We can no longer help him but what may we do to ourselves if we do not follow these instructions? _____.

Step seven: Our fate has been determined. We must live for today.

Step eight: What should we allow our memories to do? _____ Once the soul has left us, what should we do? _____

_____

Written so many years ago, I found these words a bit surprising, yet at the same time inspiring. What did you discover? _____

_____

_____

WORKS OF MERCY

Do you remember the corporal and spiritual *works of mercy*? It may be a good time to be reminded of these most charitable acts. Review the Corporal Works (left column) and the Spiritual Works (right column).

⇒ Feed the hungry   ⇒ Instruct the ignorant
⇒ Give drink to the thirsty   ⇒ Counsel the doubtful
⇒ Clothe the naked   ⇒ Admonish sinners
⇒ Visit the imprisoned   ⇒ Bear wrongs patiently
⇒ Shelter the homeless   ⇒ Forgive offenses willingly
⇒ Visit the sick   ⇒ Comfort the afflicted
⇒ Bury the dead   ⇒ Pray for the living and the dead

The corporal works of mercy speak about burying the dead. The spiritual works of mercy include: pray for the living and the dead. We bury them and then pray for them. We are instructed to aid our neighbors in both their spiritual and bodily needs throughout their lives—and even their holy deaths. The rituals and customs of death have been with us for thousands of years and the regard shown to our deceased has been handed down from generation to generation. I think it is wise to remember with clarity and to reflect on the immense respect and thoughtful prayer that accompanies someone at death. Our deaths are holy to God and our works on earth are essential.

Are these "works" really that important? James 2: 14-16 teaches candidly about them:

What good is it, my brothers, if someone says he has faith but does not have works? Can that faith save him? If a brother or sister has nothing to wear and has no food for the day, and one of you says to them, "Go in peace, keep warm, and eat well," but you do not give them the necessities of the body, what good is it?

JESUS' BURIAL

But he was pierced for our offenses, crushed for our sins, Upon him was the chastisement that makes us whole, by his stripes we were healed. We had all gone astray like sheep, each following his own way; But the LORD laid upon him the guilt of us all. Though he was harshly treated, he submitted and opened not his mouth; Like a lamb led to the slaughter or a sheep before the shearers, he was silent and opened not his mouth. Oppressed and condemned, he was taken away, and who would have thought any more of his destiny? When he was cut off from the land of the living, and smitten for the sin of his people, A grave was assigned him among the wicked and a burial place with evildoers, Though he had done no wrong nor spoken any falsehood.

This sounds like an exact recalling of the persecution and burial of Jesus, however, it was written about 700 years before Christ's birth. This passage is from Isaiah 53: 5-9 and it holds a few more pieces to the puzzle. In this foretelling of Christ's suffering, we come to understand the words pierced, chastisement, and stripes more clearly. The sentence, *But the LORD laid upon him the guilt of us all*, is so perfectly written once you understand Jesus carried, and then died upon our cross. Every sentence pivots perfectly into place as if they were tumblers to a safe. The secrets of the unlocked door were playing out live in front of Mary and now these familiar verses would hold new meaning and life. Mary's most grief-laden day would prove to carry the weight of four of her seven sorrows.

Reread it as many times as you like, taking it all in, and then spend some time with me on the last sentence beginning with...A grave.

How did he happen to get this grave? _____

Who were these graves used for? _____

Again it reminds us that Jesus DID NOT belong there. Let's think back to Mary. Oh, humble Mary! Let's say that she knew this passage of Isaiah by heart, would she still not have had a bit of tugging going on in her spirit? Burials were very important to the Jewish people. Proper ceremonies, traditions, and rituals were handed down for years and Mary would have attended many funerals over her lifetime, including most holy Joseph's. As we already know, Joseph was a righteous man so it stands to reason that, upon his death, Mary and Jesus would have highly honored his most worthy life. Therefore, on this day, it would not be easy for Mary to turn her back to tradition and custom. It would not be proper to offer this man less than he deserved. And then, to place his perfect and sinless body among the wicked would be considered a sin against God under any other circumstances. How I struggle with the irony of this day and how Mary so eloquently accepted God's Will and trusted in His Ways. Her blind faith and selflessness are duly noted. There are some major lessons here!

What do you want to remember about Mary from this sorrow? (Take your time)

_____
_____
_____
_____

FAITH IN TOMORROW

At some point, near the end of the day, Mary had to walk away from her Son. She would have to travel the streets back to her home without his company and she would know that things would never again be the same. Even upon his resurrection, he would have work to do to prepare his followers for the arrival of the Holy Spirit. The foundation of the Church and the New Covenant would need to be revealed to their hearts and leaders would need to be assigned. Time would advance very quickly now because he was no longer a man of this world ---- his heavenly body would swiftly come and then go again, like a sojourner passing through town on his way home.

Faith is what got Mary to this day and it would be her faith that would hold her this night. Faith would wake her in the morn and faith would protect her from the inevitable gossip, fear, anger, and pride that were certain to flow freely over the days that followed.

The Gossip----The town would be buzzing with gossip over Jesus. Peter's denial would no doubt fill a few ears, and Judas's body would have been found and the stories of his public betrayal would mount. Many would speak of the impostor receiving his due punishment. Townspeople and visitors would understandably be attempting to fill in the timeline and how such a thing could start and finish in a single day's time, especially to someone who had cured so many and was loved by even more.

The Fear --- Scripture indicates that fear was running rampant following Jesus' death. The evildoers who crucified Jesus would be prepared to stomp out any rekindling of his message. The chief priests and Pharisees, according to Matthew, had already planned their next step including an appeal to Pilate for a sealed and guarded tomb (remembering that Jesus had spoken of being raised from the dead). Once the Leader was out of the way, their attention would focus on his followers, and they would plot ways to silence any rebuttal. The apostles stood as open game and rightfully hid themselves for the dust to settle. They would be morally and ethically torn between continuing the truth of Christ as Our Savior and fearing the ramifications of speaking a single word of it. Confessing them now would mean a certain death to Christianity. The apostles would mentally weigh their limited options and decide that they were powerless without Jesus. What a fearful and most difficult time this was for his disciples, after Jesus' death, before his final instructions, and before the Holy Spirit.

The Anger--- Many townspeople would no doubt hold anger and resentment toward the Government and chief priests for what they did to Jesus. Impartial people would not be inclined to become disciples and followers of Christ, therefore, the devoted and faithful hearts for Jesus would need to be stirred into action. A severe division would ensue priming every open heart for the speech that would begin Christianity. Peter's audience of three thousand would certainly know anger and would spend these days growing thirsty for his message and direction.

The Pride--- In the days to follow, there would be those who would strut around town gloating of their victory and clever manipulation of Pilate. Some would silently feel apprehension about Jesus' Crucifixion, but would hide behind a mask of pride like a coward. Still others would remain coolly indifferent, proud that they could see both sides, but without an open heart they would soon slide toward the unbelievers. Each of these groups would threaten the proliferation of God's Word and muzzle its disciples. God would allow some hearts to completely harden while others would grow soft, using each heart for His glory.

APPLYING WHAT WE HAVE LEARNED

One thing that I have realized by studying Mary is that she reveals herself openly to those who seek her. We are so blessed to have our Catholic Church who reveres her and encourages us to study her life, pray to her for intervention, and call upon her graces. You and I have learned many things about Mary but it does not end there. Allowing her seeds of faith, charity, hope, and love to fall into our rich soil is where it begins. Watering these seeds and nurturing their growth inside us will forever change our outlook and it will bring us closer to God.

It is your turn to apply the lessons to a few everyday emotions and see where Mary directs your heart for response. Taking the four categories from above, create a dialog or a scenario that you believe Mary may have happened upon in these days and work it through until you are satisfied with your answer. Placing Mary in an actual setting, on the edge of the nightmare she just witnessed, allows us to soften our minds to her teaching. Give it a try! Then sit back in amazement of how much goodness you have retained from your loving teacher.

The Gossip--- _____

_____

_____

_____

_____

_____

_____

The Fear--- _____

_____

_____

_____

_____

_____

_____

The Anger--- _____

_____

_____

_____

_____

_____

_____

The Pride--- _____

_____

_____

_____

_____

Other thoughts--- _____

_____

_____

_____

Please note that there is no perfect answer to the above questions. It may be whatever Mary places on your heart at the time. Let her infinite love for God seep into your bones that we may walk in her path of humility.

For years I have meditated on these Seven Sorrows and I have noticed something very peculiar and wonderful. No matter what is going on in my life today or what is to happen to me around the corner, Mary's message is perfectly timed and evolves or changes with each new challenge or circumstance in my life. I may put the lesson to work immediately or it may take me days or weeks to understand how well my wise teacher had prepared me for the unforeseeable turn of events. Mary teaches us what we need to know when we need to know it. There is something very comforting in studying her humble love. When we find ourselves swimming in unsettled waters, look to God for his amazing grace and ask Mary to deepen our understanding and enlighten us (her 2nd grace for us) about the Divine Mysterious of the Sorrows. Within them, we will find what we need.

SUMMARY OF THE SEVENTH SORROW

I thank you for sharing this journey with me. Each sorrow reveals so many lessons pertinent to our daily lives and its message is timeless. Studying Mary's sorrows is like following a treasure map through the GREATEST BOOK OF ALL TIME. The Bible is one of the ways God speaks to us, and therefore Mary directs us to its pages as we contemplate and absorb her Seven Sorrows. Her teaching is so subtle and loving. Her ways are so gracious.

We are better for having studied her sorrows for with it we may, all the more, appreciate the joys of her faith. Mary was not an unemotional person. She was not always serious and she did not dwell in sadness. Her Sorrows stand out because they so contrast her joyfully blessed life as the mother to Jesus, wife to Saint Joseph, and as a devout Jewish girl seeking the Will of her God. Add to that daughter, cousin, friend, student, teacher, neighbor, and confidant and you have a good look at how Mary spent her days on Earth (when she wasn't praying, that is).

My prayer for you as we close this last sorrow of Jesus' burial is that you always remember the end of the story. On the third day, our Lord Jesus Christ was resurrected. The sorrows were necessary to make us worthy and the Resurrection is the path that leads us home.

Alleluia!

God Bless You

Let us pray:

Hail Mary, full of Grace. The Lord is with you.

Blessed are you among women, and blessed is the fruit of your womb, Jesus.

Holy Mary, Mother of God, pray for us sinners, now and at the hour of our death. Amen.

I invite you to continue to pray Mary's Seven Sorrows each day for the rest of your life. It has become a part of me and I am so grateful to have found this treasure. Mary has already delivered, upon my family, many of her graces: peace, enlightenment, to console, to give for asking, to defend, visibly help, and forgive. Each day, I find myself eager for this time in prayer and contemplation and simply spending time getting to know Mary. For through her love, I see and know my God.

Printed in the United States
By Bookmasters